Home Woodworking Projects
Volume 2

Complete Handyman's Library™
Handyman Club of America
Minneapolis, Minnesota

Published in 1997 by
Handyman Club of America
12301 Whitewater Drive
Minnetonka, Minnesota 55343

Published by arrangement with Cowles Creative Publishing, Inc.
ISBN 0-86573-659-6

Printed on American paper by
R. R. Donnelley & Sons Co.
99 98 97 / 5 4 3 2 1

CREDITS:
Created by: The Editors of Cowles Creative Publishing
and the staff of the Handyman Club of America
in cooperation with Black & Decker. **BLACK&DECKER**
is a trademark of Black & Decker (US), Incorporated
and is used under license.

Handyman Club of America:
  Vice President, Product Marketing: Mike Vail
  Book Marketing Director: Cal Franklin
  Book Products Development Manager: Mark Johanson
  Book Marketing Coordinator: Jay McNaughton

Contents

Introduction

One of the many delights in making a house a home is the continual search for the exact furnishing that will bring that perfect sense of comfort, function or visual appeal you desire. This is true whether you need an accent piece for the den, an accessory for the kitchen, something to solve a particular storage problem, or a kid-sized piece of furniture. What better way is there to accomplish this than to create the desired piece yourself—and save money while doing so? *Home Woodworking Projects, Volume 2,* provides an array of projects that will help you bring the perfect touch to any room in your home.

You'll even find creative additions for your vacation home, such as a cabin chair, rod and tackle center, gun cabinet and fireplace box. Other projects include a beautiful, portable wine and stemware rack, a mirrored coat rack, a blanket chest, a sports locker, a clever game table, a stylish Mission lamp, and many other furnishings to give rooms in your home personal charm and functional appeal.

For each of the creative, practical building projects in *Home Woodworking Projects, Volume 2,* you will find a complete cutting list of parts, a materials-shopping list, a detailed construction drawing, full-color photographs of the major construction steps and easy-to-follow directions that guide you through every step of the building process.

The information in this book gives do-it-yourselfers of all skill levels the power to build beautiful wood projects, and the satisfaction of creating well-made pieces inexpensively. Every project in this book can be built using only basic hand tools and portable power tools that you probably already own. And you won't need to spend hours scouring specialty woodworking stores for the materials and hardware you'll need. We used only products that are sold in most building centers and corner hardware stores to make these items.

NOTICE TO READERS

This book provides useful instructions, but we cannot anticipate all of your working conditions or the characteristics of your materials and tools. For safety, you should use caution, care, and good judgment when following the procedures described in this book. Consider your own skill level and the instructions and safety precautions associated with the various tools and materials shown. Neither the publisher nor Black & Decker® can assume responsibility for any damage to property, injury to persons, or losses incurred as a result of misuse of the information provided.

Organizing Your Worksite

Portable power tools and hand tools offer a level of convenience that is a great advantage over stationary power tools. But using them safely and conveniently requires some basic housekeeping. Whether you are working in a garage, a basement or outdoors, it is important that you establish a flat, dry holding area where you can store tools. Set aside a piece of plywood on sawhorses, or dedicate an area of your workbench for tool storage, and be sure to return tools to that area once you are finished with them. It is also important that all waste, including lumber scraps and sawdust, be disposed of in a timely fashion. Check with your local waste disposal department before throwing away any large scraps of building materials or any finishing-material containers.

Safety Tips
•Always wear eye and hearing protection when operating power tools and performing any other dangerous activities.
•Choose a well-ventilated work area when cutting or shaping wood and when using finishing products.

Tools & Materials

At the start of each project, you'll find a set of symbols showing the power tools needed to complete the work (see below). For some projects, a router table or power miter box, available at rental centers, will also be helpful. You'll also need a set of basic hand tools: a hammer, screwdrivers, tape measure, a level, a combination square, C-clamps, and pipe or bar clamps. Each project includes a shopping list of all the construction materials needed; a list of miscellaneous materials and hardware accompanies the construction drawing. When buying lumber, note that the "nominal" size of the lumber is usually larger than the actual size. For example, a 2 × 4 is actually 1½ × 3½".

Power Tools You Will Use

Circular saw *to make straight cuts. For long cuts and rip-cuts, use a straight-edge guide. Install a carbide-tipped combination blade for most projects.*

Drills: *use a cordless drill for drilling pilot holes and counterbores, and to drive screws; use an electric drill for sanding and grinding tasks.*

Jig saw *for making contoured cuts and internal cuts. Use a combination wood blade for most projects where you will cut pine, cedar or plywood.*

Power sander *to prepare wood for a finish and to smooth out sharp edges. Owning several power sanders (⅓-sheet, ¼-sheet, and belt) is helpful.*

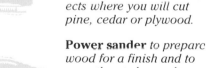

Belt sander *for resurfacing rough wood. Can also be used as a stationary sander when mounted on its side on a flat worksurface.*

Router *to cut decorative edges and roundovers in wood. As you gain more experience, use routers for cutting grooves (like dadoes) to form joints.*

Guide to Building Materials Used in This Book
•Sheet goods:
PLYWOOD: *Basic sheet good sold in several grades (from CDX to AB) and thicknesses. BCX is well-suited for outdoor projects.*
BIRCH PLYWOOD: *An alternative to pine or fir plywood, has smooth surface excellent for painting or staining. Moderately expensive.*
OAK PLYWOOD: *Oak-veneered plywood commonly sold in ¼" and ¾" thicknesses. Fairly expensive.*
LAUAN PLYWOOD: *Usually ¼" to ½" thick, found in cabinetry and furniture, and used as a flooring underlayment. Inexpensive.*
MELAMINE BOARD: *Particleboard with a glossy polymerized surface that is moisture-resistant and easy to clean. Inexpensive.*
HARDBOARD: *Dense particleboard used for backing. Inexpensive.*
PEGBOARD: *Perforated hardboard. Inexpensive.*
TILEBOARD: *Thin hardboard with a moisture-resistant surface (often with decorative patterns). Inexpensive.*

•Dimension lumber:
PINE: *A basic, versatile softwood. "Select" and "#2 or better" are suitable grades. Relatively inexpensive.*
CEDAR: *Naturally moisture-resistant softwood. Moderately expensive.*
RED OAK: *A common hardwood that stains well and is very durable. Relatively inexpensive.*
ASPEN: *A soft, workable hardwood. Moderately expensive.*

Guide to Fasteners & Adhesives Used in This Book
•Fasteners & hardware:
WOOD AND DECK SCREWS: *Brass or steel (deck screws are galvanized). Can be driven with a power driver.*
NAILS & BRADS: *Choose galvanized or brass.*
MISCELLANEOUS HARDWARE: *Door pulls and knobs, hinges, casters and other specialty hardware as required.*

•Adhesives:
WOOD GLUE: *Yellow glue is the basic wood glue.*
MOISTURE-RESISTANT WOOD GLUE: *Any exterior wood glue, such as plastic resin glue.*
TILEBOARD AND CONSTRUCTION ADHESIVE: *Sold in cartridges and applied with a caulk gun.*

•Miscellaneous materials:
Wood plugs (for filling counterbores); ceramic tile & grout; trim moldings; dowel rods; wood putty; others as required.

Finishing Your Project

Glue precut wood plugs into visible screw counterbores and sand them until smooth; fill nail holes and countersunk screw holes with wood putty, then sand smooth. Sand all surfaces to remove rough spots and splinters, using medium-grit (120- to 150-grit) sandpaper, then finish-sand (150- to 180-grit) all surfaces. Wipe the wood clean with a rag dipped in mineral spirits, then prime and paint with enamel paint, or apply a wood-staining agent to color the wood. Topcoat with several coats of tung oil, polyurethane or other products as desired. Mask or remove hardware before applying finishing products.

Cedar Bench

*The rugged simplicity of this cedar bench is well suited
for any cabin or cottage setting.*

CONSTRUCTION MATERIALS

Quantity	Lumber
3	1 × 4" × 8' cedar
2	2 × 10" × 6' cedar
1	2 × 4" × 8' cedar

This slender cedar bench has remarkably clean lines and a nice appearance, which makes it look great anywhere you put it—on a deck, in a cabin or by a backyard fire pit. A full 5 feet in length, it can seat up to three adults comfortably. Or if you prefer, it can be surrounded with other chairs or benches to do double duty as a cocktail or coffee table.

Although this cedar bench is lightweight and very simple to build, it can withstand heavy use and exposure to sun and rain. And because the construction is so simple, you can easily shorten the length to fit a special spot by shortening the 2 × 10 seat planks and the side aprons. Or, take it one step further and build the bench to a square shape for use as a one-person seat or an end table.

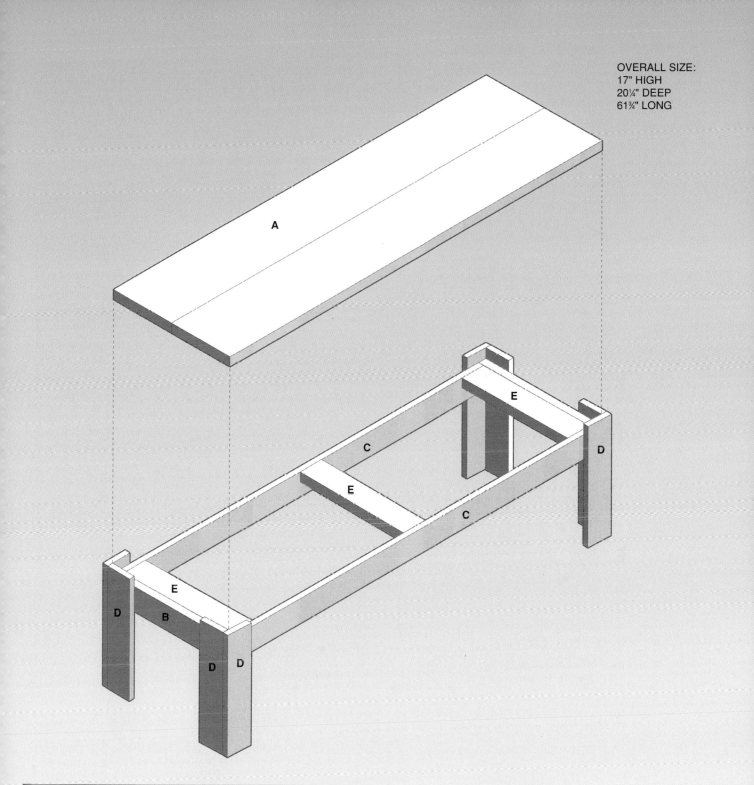

OVERALL SIZE:
17" HIGH
20¼" DEEP
61¾" LONG

A

E

C

E

D

C

E

D

B

D   D

Cutting List

Key	Part	Dimension	Pcs.	Material
A	Seat slat	1½ × 9¼ × 60"	2	Cedar
B	End apron	1½ × 3½ × 18½"	2	Cedar
C	Side apron	⅞ × 3½ × 57"	2	Cedar

Cutting List

Key	Part	Dimension	Pcs.	Material
D	Leg board	⅞ × 3½ × 17"	8	Cedar
E	Cleat	1½ × 3½ × 16¾"	3	Cedar

Materials: Moisture-resistant wood glue, deck screws (2", 2½"), ⅜"-dia. cedar plugs, finishing materials.

Note: Measurements reflect the actual thickness of dimensional lumber.

The legs are made by joining pairs of 1 × 4s at right angles.

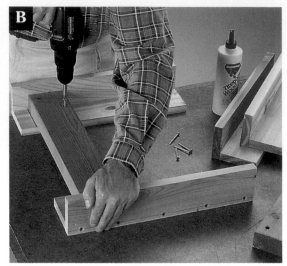

Attach the end aprons to the insides of the leg pairs, 1½" down from the tops of the legs.

Directions: Cedar Bench

MAKE THE LEGS. Each leg is made by fastening the edges of two pieces of 1 × 4 cedar together at a right angle to create an L-shape. Begin by cutting the leg boards (D) to size, and sand them to smooth out any rough edges. Butt a long edge of one leg board against a face of another leg board—since most dimensional cedar lumber is smoother on one face, be careful to keep faces of similar smoothness exposed. Join the leg-board pairs together into legs, using moisture-resistant wood glue and 2" deck screws driven through pilot holes. Be sure to counterbore the pilot holes deep enough to accept a ⅜"-dia. cedar plug (if you are not overly concerned about creating a clean, finished appearance, go ahead and drive the deck screws into pilot holes that are only countersunk slightly—just make sure the screw heads are recessed below the surface of the wood). Continue assembling the leg-board pairs until all four legs are complete **(photo A).**

ATTACH THE END APRONS. The end aprons fit between the legs at the ends of the bench. Unlike standard aprons, they are attached to the inside faces of the legs, which gives them a cleaner appearance and allows them to provide greater structural support. To minimize the number of exposed screw heads in the legs, we attached

the end aprons and side aprons by driving screws through the aprons and into the legs—this can be a little tricky because you have to be very careful how far you countersink or counterbore the pilot holes to keep the screw tips from protruding out through the faces of the legs. If you are not troubled by exposed screw heads, or

Fasten the side aprons to the insides of the legs so they are flush with the end aprons.

Fasten 1 × 4 cleats to the undersides of the seat slats to tie them together and help prevent sagging.

don't mind counterboring and plugging additional holes in the legs, then you may want to screw through the legs and into the aprons. Cut the end aprons (B) to length. Sand the ends, and set two leg pairs on your worksurface, about 21" apart. Position an end apron between the leg boards so the top edge of the apron is 1½" down from the tops of the legs. Drill countersunk pilot holes, and attach the ends with glue and 2" deck screws, driven through the ends and into the legs **(photo B).** Use plenty of moisture-resistant wood glue to reinforce the joint, and drive at least two screws into each leg board. Attach both end aprons between pairs of legs.

ATTACH THE SIDE APRONS. The 1 × 4 side aprons connect the leg/end apron assemblies. Like the end aprons, the side aprons support the seat slats on the completed bench. Cut the side aprons (C) to length. Set the leg assemblies on a flat worksurface, 57" apart. Apply glue to the ends of the side aprons, and position them between the legs, flush with the tops of the end aprons. Drive countersunk 1⅝" deck screws through the end aprons and into the legs **(photo C).**

MAKE THE SEAT. The seat for the cedar bench is simply a pair of 2 × 10s laid together edge to edge. Three cleats are attached beneath the seat slats to tie them together and help prevent sagging. Cut the seat slats (A) and cleats (E) to size. Clamp the seat slats together, edge to edge, making sure the ends are flush. Draw a reference line 1½" in from each end to mark position for the outer cleats. Set a cleat against each line, then set another in between the outer cleats. Drill pilot holes, and attach the cleats with glue and 2½" deck screws **(photo D).** Stand the leg assembly upright. Set the seat into the recess created by the tops of the aprons, and fasten it by driving 1⅝" deck screws through the aprons and into the cleats **(photo E).**

APPLY FINISHING TOUCHES. Glue ⅜"-dia. cedar wood plugs into all the counterbores in the exposed faces of the legs and aprons, then sand the plugs even with the wood after the glue dries. Finish-sand the wood surfaces, then apply your finish of choice—we used a tinted exterior wood stain.

After the seat boards are cleated together, set them on the aprons and secure them with deck screws.

Gun Cabinet

Keep hunting rifles and ammunition protected and out of sight in this spacious, locking gun cabinet.

A sturdy, clean cabinet equipped with a lock is essential for any hunting lodge or any cabin where firearms are used or stored. The gun cabinet shown here is solid and easy to make. It can hold up to four rifles, and it has six shelves with a separate locking door for storing ammunition. The board-and-batten style cabinet doors can be fit-ted with just about any kind of lock you choose, depending on your security needs. And the cabinet walls are made from solid pine, so the cabinet looks more like an armoire or pantry than an arsenal.

Structurally, this gun cabinet is basically a pine box held together with cleats on the sides and back. A center stile in front functions as a stop for the cabinet doors. The ammunition rack, built from ¾"-thick plywood, is built separately and inserted inside the cabinet, then fastened in place with wood screws.

Because the cabinet design is so simple, you can alter it to better fit your needs. For example, the ammunition rack can be eliminated, or replaced by a shelf at the top of the cabinet, to create more room for storing additional firearms. If you plan to store the cabinet in an area with high moisture, consider lining the cabinet with tileboard, then caulk the seams and corners and weatherstrip the doors to cut down on moisture penetration inside the cabinet.

CONSTRUCTION MATERIALS

Quantity	Lumber
6	1 × 2" × 8' pine
1	1 × 4" × 6' pine
6	1 × 6" × 6' pine
4	1 × 8" × 8' pine
1	¾" × 4' × 8' plywood
1	¼" × 4' × 8' lauan plywood

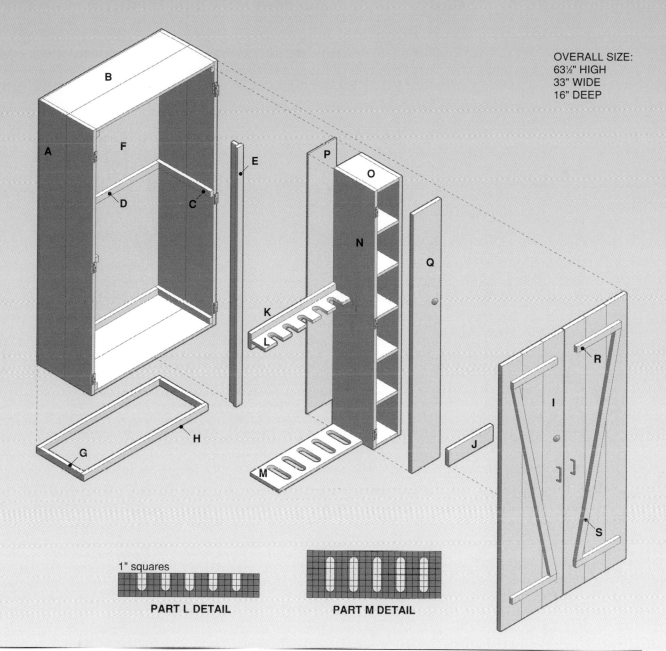

OVERALL SIZE:
63½" HIGH
33" WIDE
16" DEEP

PART L DETAIL

1" squares

PART M DETAIL

Cutting List

Key	Part	Dimension	Pcs.	Material
A	Side board	¾ × 7¼ × 62"	4	Pine
B	Top/bottom	¾ × 7¼ × 31⅝"	4	Pine
C	Side cleat	¾ × 1½ × 13¾"	6	Pine
D	Back cleat	¾ × 1½ × 31½"	3	Pine
E	Center support	¾ × 1½ × 60½"	2	Pine
F	Back	¼ × 33 × 63½"	1	Lauan plywood
G	Base frame	¾ × 1½ × 11½"	2	Pine
H	Base frame	¾ × 1½ × 33"	2	Pine
I	Door board	¾ × 5½ × 62"	6	Pine
J	Door cleat	¾ × 3½ × 12"	2	Pine

Cutting List

Key	Part	Dimension	Pcs.	Material
K	Holder back	¾ × 3½ × 23¼"	1	Pine
L	Gun holder	¾ × 4 × 23¼"	1	Plywood
M	Stock receiver	¾ × 8 × 22½"	1	Plywood
N	Storage side	¾ × 11 × 60½"	2	Plywood
O	Cross piece	¾ × 6 × 11"	7	Plywood
P	Storage back	¼ × 7½ × 60½"	1	Lauan plywood
Q	Storage door	¾ × 7½ × 60¼"	1	Plywood
R	Door batten	¾ × 1½ × 12"	4	Pine
S	Door batten	¾ × 1½ × 52"	2	Pine

Materials: Wood glue, #6 wood screws (1", 1¼", 1⅝"), utility hinges: 1½ × 1½" (3); 1½ × 2" (6), 4d finish nails, barrel locks (2), elbow catch, door pulls, finishing materials.

Note: Measurements reflect the actual size of dimensional lumber.

Directions:
Gun Cabinet

MAKE THE CABINET SIDES. The sides of the gun cabinet, like the top and bottom panels, are made from solid 1 × 8 pine boards. The boards are held together, edge to edge, with shelf cleats that are attached to the insides and function like board battens. Start by cutting the side boards (A) and side cleats (C) to size. Clamp the side boards together, edge to edge, in groups of two—make sure the ends of the boards are flush. Draw reference lines on the inside faces of the side boards to mark position for the side cleats: the lines should be drawn on the faces of the boards in each pair, ¾" in from each end and ¾" in from one long edge **(photo A).** Also draw a centerline across each set of side boards, 31" from the ends. Position the side cleats

With the boards for each cabinet side clamped together, mark reference lines for the cabinet top and bottom, and for the back cleats.

on the board pairs. The ends of the cleats should be flush with the line along the long edge to create a ¾" recess for the back-panel cleats (installed later). The two bottom cleats should be positioned with their bottom edge on the reference line, and the top cleat will have it's

top edge on the reference line. Drill countersunk pilot holes through the side cleats, and attach them with glue and #6 × 1¼" wood screws, driven through the cleats and into the side boards.

ATTACH THE TOP & BOTTOM. Back cleats are attached to the

Position the back cleats between the cabinet sides, and attach them to the side cleats.

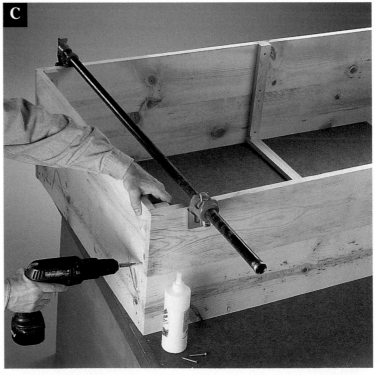

Keep the assembly stable with bar clamps, and fasten the top and bottom boards to the side cleats.

D	E

Attach the center support, making sure the front face is flush with the front edges of the cabinet.

Draw reference lines on the door panels, 5" in from each end, to mark the positions for the horizontal battens on the cabinet doors.

side cleats, connecting the cabinet sides and creating mounting surfaces for the back panel. Two top/bottom boards are then fastened to the side cleats, forming the basic cabinet carcase. Begin by cutting the top/bottom boards (B) and back cleats (D) to size. Set the back cleats between the side board assemblies, aligned with the side cleats and butted against the ends. Drill countersunk pilot holes through the back cleats, and attach them to the side cleats with glue and #6 × 1⅝" wood screws **(photo B).** With the assembly laying on its back, position two top/bottom boards between the cabinet sides at the top, and another two at the bottom. Try to make sure the seams between board pairs are aligned with the seams in the sides. Apply glue, and clamp the boards in place at each end, using a bar clamp or pipe clamp. Make sure the cabinet carcase is square, then drive wood screws through the top and bottom boards and into the side cleats **(photo C).**

MAKE THE BASE. Start by cut-

ting the base frame boards (G, H) to size. Using glue and #6 × 1⅝" wood screws, attach the base sides between the base boards, making sure the outside faces of the base sides are flush with the ends of the base boards. With the cabinet frame on its back, position the rectangular base against one end. The base should be flush with the rear and side edges of the cabinet frame. Mark the base position, and drill pilot holes through the end boards. Attach the base with glue and #6 × 1⅝" wood screws, driven through the end boards and into the base edges.

ATTACH THE BACK PANEL. The back panel for the gun cabinet is made from ¼"-thick lauan plywood. Cut the back panel (F) to size using a circular saw and a straightedge cutting guide. To make sure the back panel is square, measure diagonally from corner to corner. If the measurements are the same, the back is square—this is important because the back panel is used to square-up the cabinet carcase. Lay the

cabinet down on its front edges, and set the back over the rear edges of the side boards and the back cleats. Tack the back panel at the corners, making sure it is flush with the outside edges of the cabinet all the way around. Drive 1" wire brads every 6" into the sides and back cleats to attach the back panel.

INSTALL THE CENTER SUPPORT. The center support fits in the front of the cabinet opening, running from top to bottom, to create a stile that works as a center door stop. Cut the two center support (E) pieces from 1 × 2 pine, then butt the long edge of one board against the face of the other board to form a "T" shape. Make sure the parts are flush at the ends, then join them with glue and 4d finish nails. Turn the cabinet over on its back, and position the center support in the center of the front opening. The face of the center support assembly should be directed forward, flush with the front of the cabinet. Drill pilot holes through the top and bottom

For accuracy, use a sliding T-bevel to measure and transfer the angle where the battens meet.

Position a cross piece between the storage sides at each end of the ammunition rack, and attach the parts with glue and screws.

boards, and attach the center support with glue and two #6 × 1⅝" wood screws driven at each end **(photo D).**

MAKE THE CABINET DOORS. The cabinet doors are each made with three 1 × 6 boards fitted with 1 × 2 battens, arranged in a "Z" shape, to hold the two boards together. Begin by cutting the door boards (I), door cleats (J), and door battens (R, S). Set the door boards on your worksurface, edge-to-edge, in sets of three. Use a framing square to make sure the door boards are square and flush at their ends. Clamp each set of door boards together with pipe or bar clamps. Draw reference lines across the door boards, 5" in from each end, to mark position for the horizontal battens **(photo E).** Set the horizontal battens just inside the reference lines, centered side to side, and attach them with glue and #6 × 1¼" wood screws. Note: for a more finished appearance, drive the screws

through the back faces of the door panels and into the battens. Mark the diagonal battens to fit between opposite ends of the horizontal battens on each door: the most accurate way to do this is to use a sliding T-bevel to transfer the angle of intersection onto the battens **(photo F).** Or, if you are not too concerned about precision, you can simply lay the the vertical batten strips in position and draw cutting lines that approximately follow the inside edges of the horizontal battens. Cut the vertical batten strips along the cutting lines with a jig saw or circular saw (or a power miter saw if you own one). Attach the strips to the doors with glue and wood screws. Flip the doors over on their fronts. Center a door cleat across the back of each door, and attach it with #6 × 1" wood screws.

MAKE THE AMMUNITION RACK. The ammunition rack is built as a unit and inserted into the cabinet. Because the rack has its own door, you can equip it

with its own lock for extra protection. Begin by cutting the storage sides (N), cross pieces (O) and storage back (P) to size. Position the storage sides on-edge on a flat worksurface. Glue and clamp two cross pieces between them at each end. Turn the assembly on its side, and drive 4d finish nails through the storage sides and into the cross pieces **(photo G).** Attach the storage back with glue and wire brads. Draw reference lines on the storage sides to mark the positions of the remaining cross pieces. We marked lines every 9" up the length of the ammunition rack. Apply glue to the sides of the cross pieces, and slide them in place. Check with a square to make sure the cross pieces are square to the storage sides, and attach them with 4d finish nails. Place the ammunition rack inside the main cabinet (we positioned it on the right-hand side). Make sure it is flush against the back and one side of the cabinet. Attach it by driv-

14

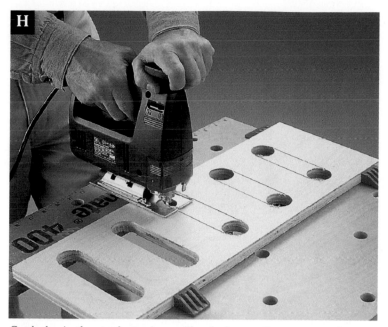
Cut holes in the stock receiver with a holesaw, then connect the holes with a jigsaw, forming notches to hold the gun stocks.

ing wood screws through the top and bottom of the cabinet and into the storage sides. Cut the storage door (Q) to size, and attach it to the innermost storage side with three 1½ × 1½" butt hinges.

MAKE THE GUN RACK. The gun rack consists of a pair of boards that are notched to hold the stock and the barrel of each gun. The boards are installed at the bottom and the center of the cabinet. Cut the gun holder (L), holder back (K) and stock receiver (M) to size from ¾"-thick plywood. Lay out the cutouts on the gun holder and stock receiver according to the *Part L Detail* and *Part M Detail* on page 79. Make the rounded ends of the cutouts with a 1½"-dia. holesaw installed in your electric drill, and use a jig saw to connect the holes, completing the cutouts **(photo H).** Sand the edges to smooth out any rough spots. Butt the gun holder against one face of the holder back. Make sure the gun

holder is centered and that the open ends of the grooves face away from the holder back. Attach the gun holder with glue and wood screws, driven through the holder back and into the gun holder edge. Fit the assembly into the cabinet, flush against the back and the middle back cleat. Glue the holder back in place, and attach it with #6 × 1" wood screws driven through the back panel and into the assembly. Position the stock receiver on the floor of the cabinet, flush against the back. Attach the stock receiver with glue and #6 × 1" wood screws.

INSTALL THE HARDWARE. Hang the cabinet doors on the cabinet with 1½ × 2" butt hinges attached to the front edges of the cabinet sides. Use three hinges for each door, positioned in the middle and about 4" in from the top and the bottom of the cabinet. We installed barrel locks in the storage door for the ammunition rack and in the cabinet door,

according to the lock manufacturer's instructions (we added an elbow catch inside the cabinet door that did not receive the barrel lock). Barrel locks are sufficient to keep young children out of the cabinets, but if higher security is important to you, use a sturdy hasp and padlock instead. Also attach door pulls to each cabinet door (because we installed a barrel lock on the ammunition rack door, we didn't feel that a pull was necessary—if you do not install a lock, cut a finger grip slot in the door with your jig saw).

APPLY FINISHING TOUCHES. Set all nail heads with a nail set, then fill all the screw and nail holes with wood putty. After it dries, sand the putty level with the surrounding wood. Finish-sand all the wood surfaces with medium grit, then fine grit sandpaper. Wipe with a rag dipped in mineral spirits, then apply your finish of choice after the wood dries. We simply applied two coats of water-based polyurethane for a protective coat that hardens the wood. If you prefer to paint your gun cabinet, be sure to use primer and a good-quality enamel paint. To protect your guns while they are in the cabinet, cut strips of felt and glue them around the cutouts in the gun holder and stock receiver, using contact cement. A layer of felt at the bottom of each stock receiver cutout is also a good idea. For best results and maximum safety, find a cool, dry and well-protected area to keep your gun cabinet. Do not place it near heat sources or in high traffic areas.

Overjohn

Convert wasted space above your toilet into usable storage with this compact "overjohn" shelving unit.

It wasn't long ago that few people had ever heard the term "overjohn," but that is changing quickly. An overjohn is a storage unit that fits against the wall above a toilet—a space that is seldom put to good use even in the tiniest bathrooms. Many overjohn cabinets being installed today provide useful storage, but they are heavy and bulky, and they cause the bathroom to look

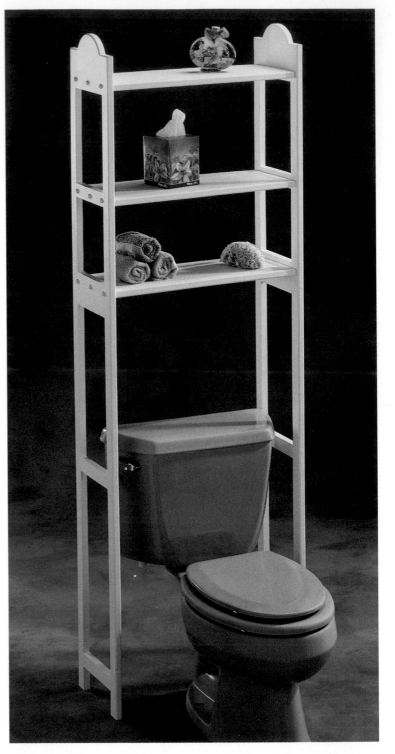

smaller than it actually is. Because the design featured here is open-sided, it has a lightweight, airy appearance that melts into the background virtually unnoticed. Yet our overjohn is spacious enough to accommodate enough towels and linens for an entire family.

This overjohn shelving unit will function as a freestanding unit under normal conditions. But if you plan to store heavier items in it, or have an unusually large volume of traffic through the bathroom, add a cleat to the back of the unit and attach it to the wall.

CONSTRUCTION MATERIALS

Quantity	Lumber
5	1 × 2" × 6' pine
1	1 × 4" × 4' pine
1	1 × 6" × 4' pine
1	1 × 10" × 8' pine

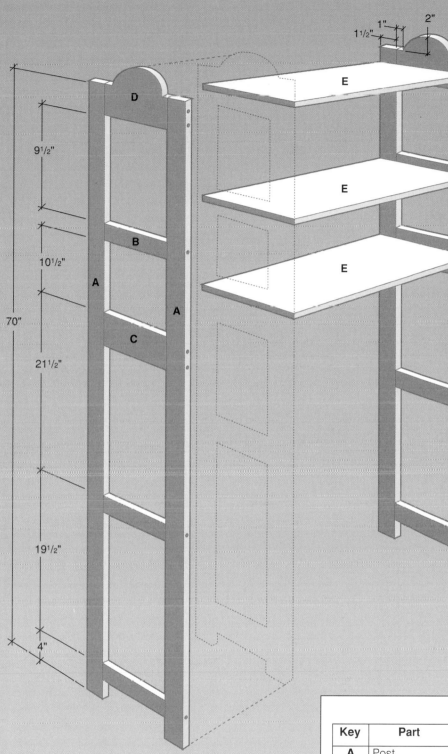

1"
1½"
2"

D

9½"

B

A
A

C

70"

10½"

21½"

19½"

4"

OVERALL SIZE:
72" HIGH
10" WIDE
23½" LONG

E

E

E

Cutting List

Key	Part	Dimension	Pcs.	Material
A	Post	¾ × 1½ × 70"	4	Pine
B	Stretcher	¾ × 1½ × 7"	6	Pine
C	Middle stretcher	¾ × 3½ × 7"	2	Pine
D	Cap stretcher	¾ × 5½ × 7"	2	Pine
E	Shelf	¾ × 9¼ × 22"	3	Pine

Materials: Wood glue, wood plugs, wood screws (#8 × 1½",
#8 × 2½").

Note: Measurements reflect the actual size of dimensional
lumber.

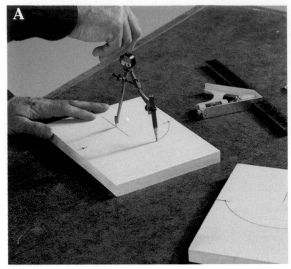

Using a compass, lay out a curved cutting line with a 2½" radius at the top of each cap stretcher.

Mark the stretcher positions, according to the detail diagram, on the posts using a combination square.

Directions: Overjohn

MAKE THE FRAME COMPONENTS. Start by cutting all of the frame components to size. Cut the posts (A) and the stretchers (B) to length from 1 × 2 pine. Cut the middle stretchers (C) to length from 1 × 4 pine and cut the cap stretchers (D) to length from 1 × 6 pine. Following the dimensions in the *Diagram*, page 17, use a compass to lay out a curved cutting line with a 2½" radius at the top of each cap stretcher **(photo A).** Cut out the curved contours with a jig saw.

ASSEMBLE THE FRAME. Lay the posts on edge on a flat worksurface and clamp them together. Following the *Diagram*, lay out the stretcher positions on the posts and, using a combination square, scribe reference lines across all of the posts **(photo B).** While the posts are still clamped together, drill pilot holes through the posts for the screws. Position the holes according to the *Dia-*

Drill pilot holes through the posts at the stretcher locations.

gram **(photo C).** Unclamp the posts, turn them over and drill counterbore holes for pine plugs. Now, lay the posts flat on the worksurface with the stretcher layout lines facing each other. Be sure to keep the bottoms of the posts at the same end to keep the stretcher positions lined up. Apply glue to the ends of the stretchers, then place the stretchers in their appropriate locations and fasten to the sides with #8 × 2½" wood screws. When both frames are assembled, insert

pine plugs into the counterbore holes using wood glue and a hammer. Sand the plugs so they are level with the wood surface. Using a router with a ⅜" piloted roundover bit, shape the edges and top end on each frame assembly, rounding over from both sides **(photo D).** Sand the frames with medium (100- or 120-grit) sandpaper to smooth out rough spots, then finish-sand with fine (150- or 180-grit) sandpaper.

TIP

Make sure that any overjohn storage unit you build or purchase doesn't restrict access to the tank and plumbing of your toilet. Measure your toilet to make sure that the overjohn allows at least 12" of clearance above the tank top, and 3" of free space at each side.

Round over the edges of the frame assembly using a router and ⅜" piloted roundover bit.

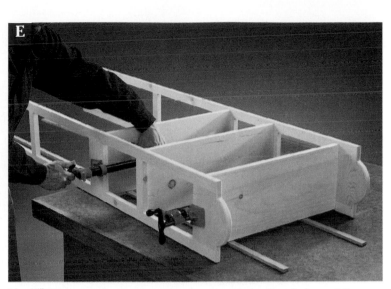

Use ¼"-thick wood spacers to create a recess for the shelves at the front of the overjohn.

BUILD & INSTALL THE SHELVES. Cut the shelves (E) to size from 1 × 10 pine. Using a router with a ⅜" piloted roundover bit, shape both edges of each shelf, rounding over from both sides. Lay the frame assemblies on a flat surface and lay out the inside of both frame assemblies for the shelf positions, according to the dimensions on the *Diagram* on page 17. Then, drill three pilot holes at each shelf location. Turn the frame assemblies over and drill counterbores at the pilot hole locations, for mushroom-style button plugs. With the shelf positions marked and drilled, apply glue to the ends of a shelf, place the frame assemblies on their back edge, and position the first shelf. It doesn't matter which shelf you install first. Place two ¼"-thick strips of wood between the worksurface and the shelf edge to provide the proper spacing for the front shelf recess. Clamp the shelf and frame assemblies together **(photo E),** being careful not to overtighten the clamps, which could squeeze the glue right out of the joint. Screw the frame assemblies to the shelf with #8 × 1½" screws, then remove the clamps. Repeat the steps for the remaining shelves.

APPLY FINISHING TOUCHES. Scrape away any excess glue with a chisel or scraper, then finish-sand the entire overjohn unit with fine sandpaper. Apply the finish as desired. We painted the overjohn, then applied two coats of satin-gloss polyurethane over the paint for extra moisture protection. You may prefer to use stain and a water-resistant topcoat instead. When the finish is dry, fill all open counterbore holes by gluing mushroom-style button plugs in place **(photo F).** Wipe up any excess glue with a wet cloth. If you want to fasten the overjohn to a wall, simply install a 1 × 4 wall cleat between the side assemblies under the bottom shelf and drill counterbored pilot holes. Finish the cleat to match the overjohn, and fasten it to the wall with screws driven through the cleat and into wall framing member locations. If there are no wall framing members in the area behind the toilet, use toggle bolts to attach the cleat.

Fill all open counterbore holes with mushroom-style button plugs. Apply glue and install with a hammer.

Knickknack Shelf

Add some country charm to your home with this rustic pine knickknack shelf.

CONSTRUCTION MATERIALS

Quantity	Lumber
1	1 × 4" × 8' pine
2	1 × 8" × 8' pine
1	1 × 10" × 4' pine
9	¼ × 3½" × 3' beaded pine paneling
1	¾ × ¾" × 6' cove molding

Country-style furniture is becoming increasingly popular throughout the world because of its honest appearance and back-to-basics preference for function over ornate styling. In fancy interior design catalogs, you may find many country shelving projects that are similar to this one in design and function. But our knickknack shelf can be built for a tiny fraction of the prices charged for its catalog cousins.

From the beaded pine paneling to the matching arcs on the apron and ledger, this knickknack shelf is well designed throughout. The shelf shown above has a natural wood finish, but it is also suitable for decorative painting techniques, like milkwash or farmhouse finishes.

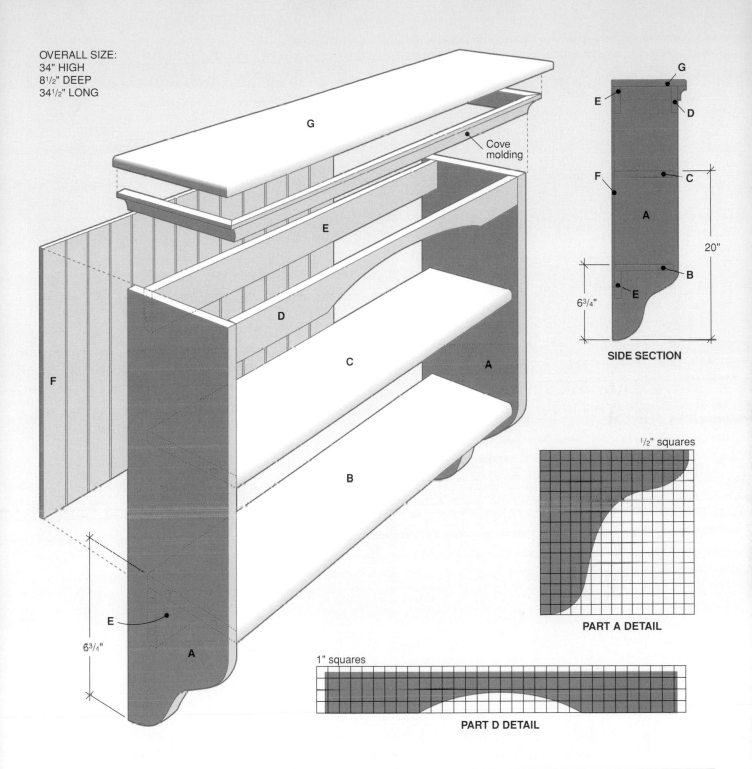

OVERALL SIZE:
34" HIGH
8¹/₂" DEEP
34¹/₂" LONG

G

Cove molding

SIDE SECTION

G

E

D

F

C

A

B

E

20"

6³/₄"

F

E

D

C

A

B

E

A

6³/₄"

¹/₂" squares

PART A DETAIL

1" squares

PART D DETAIL

Cutting List				
Key	Part	Dimension	Pcs.	Material
A	Shelf side	¾ × 7¼ × 33¼"	2	Pine
B	Bottom shelf	¾ × 6¾ × 30½"	1	Pine
C	Middle shelf	¾ × 6¾ × 30½"	1	Pine
D	Apron	¾ × 3½ × 30½"	1	Pine

Cutting List				
Key	Part	Dimension	Pcs.	Material
E	Ledger	¾ × 3½ × 30½"	2	Pine
F	Back panel	¼ × 3½ × 28"	9	Pine paneling
G	Cap	¾ × 8½ × 34½"	1	Pine

Materials: Wood glue, #8 × 1⅝" wood screws, 3d and 6d finish nails, mushroom-style button plugs, finishing materials.

Note: Measurements reflect the actual thickness of dimensional lumber.

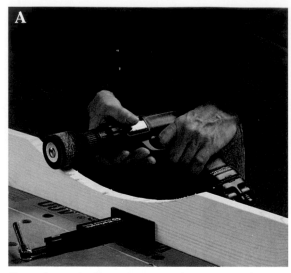

Smooth out the jig saw cuts on the apron and ledger with a drill and drum sander.

Clamp the sides and ledgers in position, then fasten with glue and screws.

Directions: Knickknack Shelf

MAKE THE FRAME COMPONENTS. Start by cutting the sides (A) to length from 1 × 8 pine. Transfer the pattern for the sides (see *Diagram*): draw a grid with ½" squares on one of the sides, then draw the profile shown in the pattern, using the grid as a reference. Cut out the shape and smooth the cut with a drum sander attached to your drill. Trace the finished profile onto the other side, and make the cutout.

Cut the apron (D) and the ledgers (E) to length from 1 × 4 pine. Use the same technique to draw and cut out the apron and one of the ledgers (see *Diagram*). Smooth out any irregularities with a drum sander or belt sander **(photo A).**

ASSEMBLE THE FRAME. Stand the sides on their back edges and place the upper ledger between them, with

Fasten the tongue-and-groove beaded pine panel pieces to the ledgers with 3d finish nails.

the top edges flush. Place a ¼" spacer under the ledger to create a recess for the back panel. Clamp the sides and ledger together with a pipe or bar clamp.

Insert the lower ledger with its top edge 6" up from the bottoms of the sides, also resting on ¼" spacers. Clamp in place, and drill two counterbored pilot holes through the sides into the ends of the ledgers. Attach the sides to the ledgers

with glue and wood screws **(photo B).**

INSTALL THE BACK PANEL & APRON. To make the back panel (F), we used tongue-and-groove pieces of pine wainscoting paneling, joined together and trimmed to create a 30½ × 28" panel.

Attach the back panel to the backs of the ledgers, using 3d finish nails, but no glue **(photo C).** The top of the back panel should be flush with the tops of the sides.

Fasten the apron across the top front of the sides with wood glue and 6d finish nails. Be sure to keep the top edge of the apron flush with the tops of the sides.

BUILD & INSTALL THE SHELVES. Cut the bottom shelf (B) and middle shelf (C) to size from 1 × 8 pine. Using a router with a ⅜" piloted roundover bit, round over the top and bottom edges on the fronts of the shelves **(photo D).**

Clamp the bottom shelf in place on top of the lower ledger, keeping the back edges flush. Drill counterbored pilot holes, and attach the shelf with glue and wood screws. Install the middle shelf using the same procedure **(photo E).**

ATTACH THE CAP & COVE. Cut the cap (G) to size from 1 × 10 pine. Using a router with a ⅜" roundover bit, shape the top and bottom edges of the ends and front. Place a bead of glue along the top edges of the shelf sides, apron and ledgers. Position the cap on top of the shelf assembly, overlapping 1¼" on each end and at the front. Nail the cap in place with 6d finish nails.

Cut the pine cove molding to the appropriate lengths with mitered corners, and attach just below the bottom of the cap (see *Diagram*). Fasten in place with glue and 3d finish nails **(photo F).**

APPLY FINISHING TOUCHES. Decide where to hang the knickknack shelf, and drill counterbored pilot holes in the upper ledger for mounting screws. Scrape off any excess glue, then finish-sand. Install mushroom-style button plugs in all counterbores, then apply the finish. We chose to finish our knickknack shelf with light oak stain and a satin-gloss polyurethane topcoat.

Use a router with a ⅜" piloted roundover bit to shape the front edges of the shelves.

Drill counterbored pilot holes for the shelves, then attach with glue and 1½" wood screws.

Attach the cove molding with glue and 3d finish nails. Hold the nails with needlenose pliers when nailing in hard-to-reach areas.

Wine & Stemware Cart

This solid oak cart with a lift-off tray allows you to safely transport and serve your wine, and provides an elegant place to display your vintage selections.

CONSTRUCTION MATERIALS

Quantity	Lumber
2	1 × 12" × 6' oak
1	1 × 4" × 8' oak
1	1 × 4" × 6' oak
1	1 × 2" × 4' oak
1	½ × 2¾" × 2' oak*
1	½ × 3¾" × 4' oak*

*Available at woodworking supply stores.

With our versatile oak wine and stemware cart, you can display, move and serve wine and other cordials from one convenient station. This cart can store up to 15 bottles of wine, liquor, soda or mix, and it holds the bottles in the correct downward position to prevent wine corks from drying out.

The upper stemware rack holds more than a dozen long-stemmed wine or champagne glasses, and a removable serving tray with easy-to-grip handles works well for cutting cheese and for serving drinks and snacks. Beneath the tray is a handy storage area for napkins, corkscrews and other utensils. Sturdy swivel casters make this wine rack fully mobile over tile, vinyl or carpeting.

OVERALL SIZE:
40³/₈" HIGH
23¹/₂" WIDE
11¹/₄" DEEP

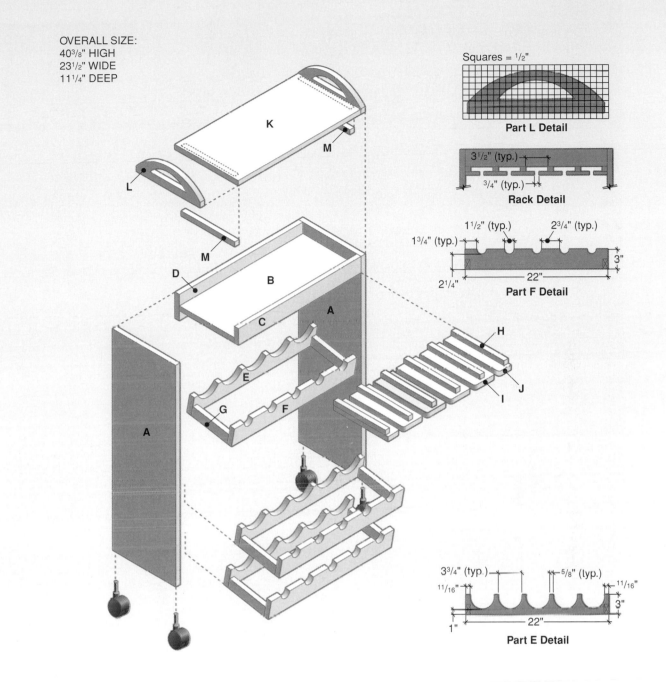

Squares = ¹/₂"

Part L Detail

3¹/₂" (typ.)

³/₄" (typ.)

Rack Detail

1¹/₂" (typ.)   2³/₄" (typ.)

1³/₄" (typ.)

2¹/₄"

22"

3"

Part F Detail

3³/₄" (typ.)   ⁵/₈" (typ.)

11/16"   11/16"

1"   22"   3"

Part E Detail

Key	Part	Dimension	Pcs.	Material
A	Side	¾ × 11¼ × 34"	2	Oak
B	Top	¾ × 9¾ × 22"	1	Oak
C	Front stretcher	¾ × 2½ × 22"	1	Oak
D	Back stretcher	¾ × 4 × 22"	1	Oak
E	Wine rack, back	¾ × 3 × 22"	3	Oak
F	Wine rack, front	¾ × 3 × 22"	3	Oak
G	Wine rack, cleat	¾ × 1½ × 6½"	6	Oak

Cutting List

Key	Part	Dimension	Pcs.	Material
H	Stemware slat	¾ × ¾ × 9¼"	6	Oak
I	Stemware plate	½ × 3½ × 9¾"	4	Oak
J	End plate	½ × 2⅛ × 9¾"	2	Oak
K	Tray	¾ × 11¼ × 22"	1	Oak
L	Tray handle	¾ × 3½ × 11¼"	2	Oak
M	Tray feet	¾ × ¾ × 9½"	2	Oak

Cutting List

Materials: Wood glue, #6 wood screws (1", 1¼"), casters (4), finishing materials.

Note: Measurements reflect the actual thickness of dimensional lumber.

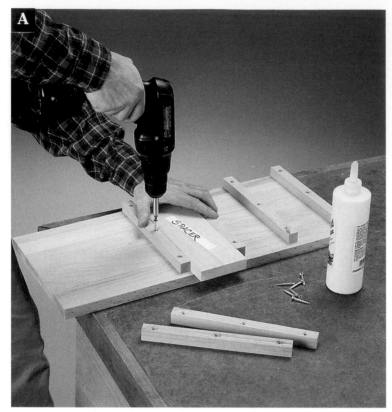

Use a spacer to keep the slats aligned properly, and attach with glue and countersunk screws.

Use a drum sander attached to your portable drill to smooth the curved jig saw cuts on each rack.

Directions: Wine and Stemware Cart

CONSTRUCT THE SIDES AND STEMWARE RACK ASSEMBLY. Start by cutting the cart sides (A), top (B) and back stretcher (D) from 1 × 12 oak. Cut the front stretcher (C) from 1 × 3 oak, and stemware slats (H) from 1 × 4 oak. Cut the plates (I) and end plates (J) to size from ½"-thick oak. Clamp a belt sander perpendicular to your worksurface, and round over the front corners of the stemware plates, as well as one corner of each end plate. Sand the remaining cut edges smooth with an orbital sander.

Next, position the top face-down, and arrange the slats on the top, flush against the back edge and evenly spaced 3½" apart (use a piece of scrap wood as a spacer). Keep the outer slats flush with the edges of the top. Drill countersunk pilot holes and attach the cleats to the underside of the top piece with glue and 1¼" screws **(photo A).**

CUT AND ASSEMBLE THE WINE RACKS. The wine racks are first assembled as individual units, and are then attached to the sides of the cart.

Cut the wine rack backs (E) and fronts (F) from 1 × 4 oak, and cut the cleats (G) from 1 × 2 oak. Transfer the pattern for the wine rack backs and fronts to each piece (see *Diagram*) and cut them out carefully with a jig saw.

Position the cleats between the fronts and backs of the wine racks, and drill two counterbored pilot holes through the fronts and backs and into the ends of the cleats at each corner. Join the pieces with glue and 1¼" screws, checking to make sure the wine racks are square. Plug the counterbores with glued wood plugs. Clamp each completed rack to

*Measure ½" along front and 2½" along back of each side, and con-
nect marks for bottom rack alignment.*

*Clamp a 4 × 10" spacer between the bottom and
middle rack for proper position. Repeat for top rack.*

*Drive screws through pilot holes in slats to secure top to sides. Coun-
terbore holes through the sides into the top edges, and drive additional screws to secure the top in place.*

your worksurface, and sand the
curves smooth with a drum
sander **(photo B).** Use an orbital sander to smooth the
plugs, and any other rough
edges.

ATTACH THE WINE RACKS TO
THE CART. The racks are installed at a slight angle, to
ensure that the wine in each
bottle will be in constant contact with the cork. This keeps

the corks moist and helps prevent them from cracking and
spoiling the wine.

On the inside face of each
side piece, measure up ⅛" from
the bottom and make a mark
along the front edge. Measure
up 2½" from the bottom and
make a mark along the back
edge. Draw an angled reference line between the marks
(photo C). With one of the
side pieces lying flat on your
worksurface, position the first
wine rack so the bottom edge
is flush against the reference
line and the front edge is set
back ¾" from the front edge of
the side piece. Drill countersunk pilot holes and attach the
rack to the side with glue and
1¼" screws.

Attach the middle rack and
top rack in the same manner,

using a 4 × 10" spacer to position them correctly **(photo D).**

Using bar clamps, position the opposite side piece, and arrange the stretchers in place between the sides. Check to make sure the unattached cleats are at the proper position and that the stretchers are flush with the top edges of the cabinet. Drill counterbored pilot holes, then use glue and 1¼" screws to anchor the stretchers and remaining cleats. Check frequently during assembly to make sure the cabinet is square.

ATTACH THE TOP ASSEMBLY. Lay the cart on its side, and clamp the top between the side pieces. The bottom face of the top should be flush with the bottom edge of the front stretcher. Drill three evenly spaced horizontal pilot holes through the outer slats into the sides, then use glue and screws to fasten the top to the sides from inside the cart **(photo E).** Drill three evenly spaced counterbored pilot holes through the stretchers into the edges of the top, and secure with glue and 1¼" screws.

To complete the stemware rack, position the cabinet upside down. Center the stemware plates over the slats, with the square end flush against the back stretcher, then drill three evenly spaced counterbored pilot holes along the center of each plate. Attach the plates to the slats with glue and 1"

For consistent placement of the stemware racks, use a ¾" spacer to position the bottom plates on the slats.

TIP

Jig saw blades cut on the upward stroke, so the top side of the workpiece may tear. To protect the finished or exposed side of a project, cut with this side facedown. This way, if the blade tears, it will remain hidden on the unexposed side. Remember to use a faster blade speed if you are cutting with a coarse-tooth blade. When cutting curves, a narrow blade is recommended. Move the saw slowly to avoid bending the blade. Some jig saws have a scrolling knob that allows the blade to be turned without turning the saw.

screws **(photo F).** Attach the end plates to the outside slats with glue and 1" nails driven through counterbored pilot holes.

While the cart is still upside down, drill holes into the bottom edges of the cart sides, and test-fit the casters **(photo G).**

MAKE THE TRAY. The wine cart tray is simply a flat oak board with handles attached to the sides and narrow feet attached below.

While the cart is upside down, drill the bottom edges of the sides for casters.

Drill a pilot hole and then cut the inside handle profile with a jig saw. Use scrap wood to support the workpiece and prevent tearouts.

Cut the tray bottom (K) from 1 × 12 oak, and cut the tray handle blanks (L) from 1 × 4 oak. Also cut the ¾ × ¾" feet (M). Mark the pattern for the handles on the blank (see *Diagram*). Drill a starter hole on the inside portion of the handle, then use a jig saw to cut along the pattern lines **(photo H).**

Position the tray between the handles, then drill three evenly spaced counterbored pilot holes through the edge of each handle. Attach the handles to the tray with glue and 1¼" screws.

Position the tray feet ⅛" in from the sides of the tray bottom and ⅞" from the front and back. Drill counterbored pilot holes, then attach the feet with glue and 1" screws.

APPLY THE FINISHING TOUCHES. Glue ⅜" oak plugs into each counterbore, and sand the plugs flush. Sand the entire cart to 150-grit smoothness, and finish with your choice of stain (we used a rustic oak), and polyurethane topcoat. NOTE: If you will be using the tray as a cutting board, make sure to use a nontoxic finish. When the finish is dry, install the casters on the bottom of the cart.

TIPS

Brushing on a thin coat of sanding sealer before you apply wood stain will help the wood absorb stain more evenly and can eliminate blotchy finishes. Sanding sealer is a clear product, usually applied with a brush. Check the backs of the product labels on all the finishing products you plan to apply to make sure they are compatible.

Behind-the-sofa Bookcase

This efficient bookcase fits right behind your sofa or up against a wall to provide display space and a trimmed-out tabletop surface.

CONSTRUCTION MATERIALS

Quantity	Lumber
2	1 × 10" × 8' aspen
1	1 × 8" × 8' aspen
3	1 × 4" × 8' aspen
2	1 × 2" × 8' aspen
2	1 × 3" × 8' chair rail molding

The space behind your sofa may not be the first area that comes to mind when you're searching for extra storage, but it does hold many possibilities for the space-starved home. This clever behind-the-sofa bookcase has display space below and a spacious tabletop that combine to make one slick

wood project. The tabletop is high enough so it can be used as an auxiliary coffee table, if you don't mind reaching up for your beverage or snack.

We used aspen to build this table, then stained it for a natural appearance. If you prefer, you can build it from pine and paint it to match or complement your sofa.

OVERALL SIZE:
34" HIGH
9¼" DEEP
59" LONG

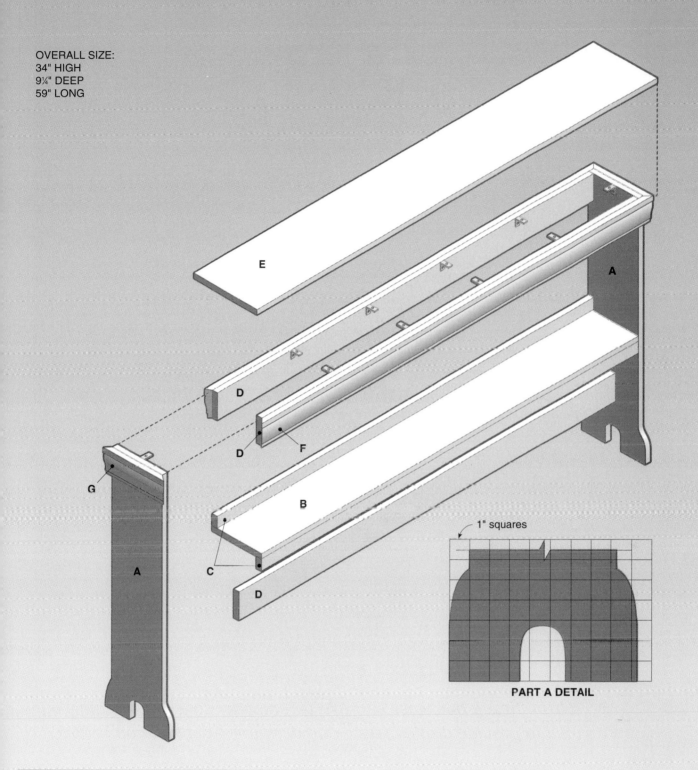

1" squares

PART A DETAIL

Cutting List

Key	Part	Dimension	Pcs.	Material
A	Leg	¾ × 9¼ × 33¼"	2	Aspen
B	Shelf	¾ × 7¼ × 55½"	1	Aspen
C	Shelf rail	¾ × 1½ × 55½"	2	Aspen
D	Stretcher	¾ × 3½ × 55½"	3	Aspen

Cutting List

Key	Part	Dimension	Pcs.	Material
E	Tabletop	¾ × 9¼ × 59"	1	Aspen
F	Face trim	¾ × 2¼ × *"	2	Molding
G	End trim	¾ × 2¼ × *"	2	Molding

Materials: Wood glue, wood screws (#6 × 1¼", #6 × 2", #8 × ½"), 1¼" brass brads, 1½" corner braces (10), finishing materials.

Note: Measurements reflect the actual size of dimensional lumber.
*Cut to fit

Directions:
Behind-the-sofa Bookcase

MAKE THE LEGS. The legs for the bookcase are cut to shape with a jig saw. They feature decorative cutouts at the bottoms to add some style and to create feet that help with stabilization. Cut the legs (A) to the full size listed in the *Cutting List*, using 1 × 10 wood. Use the Part A Detail pattern on page 31 as a reference for laying out the cutting lines to form the feet at the bottoms of the legs. You may want to draw a 1"-square grid pattern at the bottom of one of the legs first. The safest way to make sure the shapes of the legs match is to cut one first, then use it as a template for tracing the shape for the second leg. Lay out the leg shape on one leg, using a straightedge to make sure the 1" relief cuts that run all the way up the edges of the legs are straight. Cut the straight section of one leg with a circular saw and a straightedge guide, and cut the patterned bottom with a jig saw. Sand the edges smooth, then trace the profile and cut the other leg **(photo A)**.

ATTACH THE SHELF & RAILS. The rails are attached to the front and back of the shelf to add strength and to create a lip in back so display items don't fall between the bookcase and the sofa. The front shelf rail fits

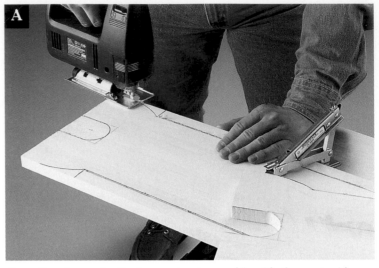

Draw the shapes for the legs onto pieces of 1 × 10, then cut with a jig saw. Make the long straight cuts with a circular saw.

Attach the shelf by driving wood screws through counterbored pilot holes in the legs.

up against the bottom of the shelf, flush with the front edge. The rear shelf rail fits on the top of the shelf, flush with the back edge. Cut the shelf (B) and shelf rails (C) to size, and sand the sharp edges slightly. Drill rows of pilot holes for #6 × 1¼" wood screws ⅜" in from the front and back edges of the shelf, for attaching the rails. Space the pilot holes at 8" intervals, then counterbore each pilot hole to accept a ⅜"-dia. wood plug. Make sure to drill the rows of counterbores on

opposite faces of the shelf from one another. Apply glue to the top edge of one rail, and clamp it to the shelf, making sure the front of the rail is flush with the edge of the shelf. Drive #6 × 1¼" wood screws through the counterbored pilot holes to secure the rail. Then, attach the other rail to the opposing face of the shelf. To attach the shelf and rails to the legs, first use a combination square to mark guidelines across one face of each leg, 16" up from the bottom. Drill pilot holes ⅜" down from

TIP

Crown molding is the molding type most frequently installed at the joints between walls and ceilings, but it also works well for trimming out the tops of cabinets, tables and other furnishings. Because it slopes downward when installed, making perfect joints can be a little tricky. Practice on some small scraps before you cut the actual trim pieces.

Use 1½" corner braces and ½" wood screws to attach the tabletop to the stretchers and the insides of the legs.

the guidelines, and counterbore the pilot holes. Apply glue to the ends of the shelf and rails, and position them between the legs so the top of the shelf is flush with the guidelines. Secure the shelf by driving #6 × 2" screws through the legs and into the shelf ends **(photo B).** Allow the glue to dry, and remove the clamps.

ATTACH THE STRETCHERS. Three stretchers fit between the legs at the bottom and top of the project to add strength and stability. A single lower stretcher is centered on the legs, while the top stretchers fit flush against the front and rear edges. The top stretchers anchor the tabletop. Begin by cutting the stretchers (D) to size. Before attaching the stretchers, carefully mark their positions on the inside faces of the legs. Center one stretcher 6" up from the bottoms of the legs, and attach it with glue and counterbored #6 × 2" wood screws, driven through the legs and into the stretcher ends. Attach the remaining two stretchers at the tops of the legs, flush with the front, top and back edges.

ATTACH THE TABLETOP. The tabletop is attached to the leg assembly with 1½" brass corner braces. Once the top is fastened, molding is cut to fit and attached to the top stretchers and legs, completing the sofa table. Start by cutting the tabletop (E) to size. Sand the top with medium-grit sandpaper to smooth out the edges. Turn the leg assembly upside down, and position it on the underside of the tabletop. Center the legs to create a 1" overhang at all sides. Clamp the legs to the tabletop, and use #8 × ½" wood screws and corner braces (four per side, one per end) to

secure the legs and stretchers to the tabletop **(photo C).**

INSTALL THE TRIM. The trim pieces that wrap the tabletop are cut from 3" crown molding, installed with mitered corner joints. Cut a piece of crown molding to about 64" in length to use for one face trim (F) piece, then place it against an edge of the tabletop and mark the ends of the tabletop onto the molding. Make 45° miter cuts away from the marks, then tack the piece in place with 4d finish nails. Cut the other long trim piece to the same size, and tack it in place. Use these pieces as references for cutting the end trim (G) pieces to fit. Remove the trim pieces, then refasten them with glue and 1¼"-long brads driven at regular intervals **(photo D).** Drive two brads through each joint to lock-nail the mating trim pieces together.

APPLY FINISHING TOUCHES. Glue ⅜"-dia. wood plugs into all counterbores, fill nail holes with wood putty and sand smooth. Finish-sand the bookcase with 180- or 220-grit sandpaper, then apply your selected finish. We used mahogany-tone wood stain and two coats of polyurethane.

Wrap the edges of the tabletop with trim pieces made from 3" crown molding.

Table/Chair

Based on a design from Colonial America, this clever furnishing features a tabletop that can be raised to form a backrest for a sturdy armchair.

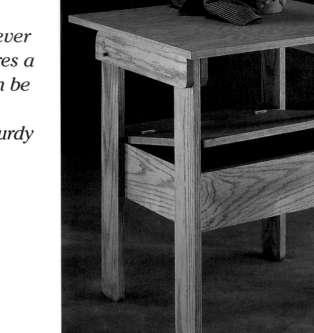

Living space was a valuable commodity in the tiny cottages of Colonial America. One clever solution they devised to solve the space crunch was the unique table/chair. With a tabletop that flipped up to do double duty as a backrest, the table/chair was a prime example of multifunctional design.

The updated version of the table/chair offered here has the same sturdy construction and multifunctional use as the original, although there are a few key differences you'll appreciate. Most notably, the tabletops of the majority of the original table/chairs were round. If your aim is to make as authentic a reproduction as possible, you can certainly build your own table/chair that way. But the difficulty of creating a perfectly round tabletop, together with the greatly increased wall space covered by the tabletop when raised, make the square version shown here an easier, less space-consuming project for most people. This table/chair design has the added

bonus of a generous storage compartment below the table shelf. And the fact that the broad surfaces in this furnishing are made from oak plywood makes it much easier to build than if you edge-glued pine boards together, as you likely would to make the original Colonial version.

CONSTRUCTION MATERIALS

Quantity	Lumber
1	1 × 6" × 8' oak
3	1 × 4" × 8' oak
1	¾" × 4 × 8' oak plywood
1	¾"-dia. × 12" oak dowel
1	⅜"-dia. × 12" oak dowel

OVERALL SIZE:
28⅝" HIGH
26⅛" WIDE
24" DEEP

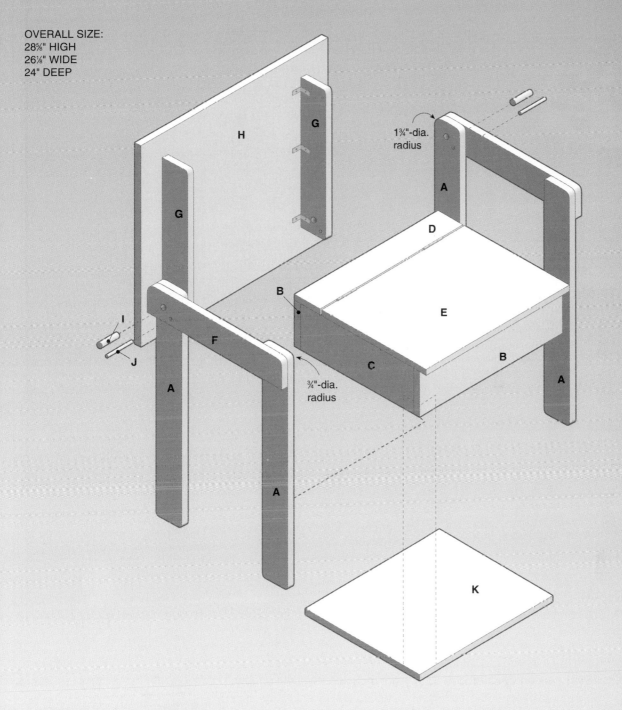

1¾"-dia. radius

¾"-dia. radius

	Cutting List						Cutting List			
Key	**Part**	**Dimension**	**Pcs.**	**Material**	**Key**	**Part**	**Dimension**	**Pcs.**	**Material**
A	Leg	¾ × 3½ × 28"	4	Oak	**G**	Table cleat	¾ × 3½ × 18"	2	Oak
B	Box side	¾ × 5½ × 20"	2	Oak	**H**	Tabletop	¾ × 24 × 26"	1	Plywood
C	Box end	¾ × 5½ × 15¾"	2	Oak	**I**	Pivot	¾"-dia. × 2¼"	2	Oak dowel
D	Hinge cleat	¾ × 3½ × 20"	1	Oak	**J**	Lock pin	⅜"-dia. × 3½"	2	Oak dowel
E	Seat	¾ × 14½ × 19¾"	1	Plywood	**K**	Box bottom	¾ × 15¾ × 18½"	1	Plywood
F	Armrest	¾ × 3½ × 18"	2	Oak					

Materials: Wood glue, #6 wood screws (1", 1¼", 2"), 3 × 1½" brass hinges (2), brass corner braces (6), ¾" oak veneer edge tape (25'), 4d finish nails, finishing materials, paste wax.

Note: Measurements reflect the actual size of dimensional lumber.

35

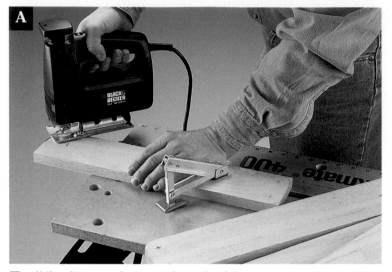

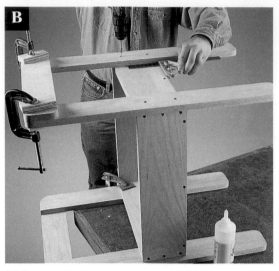

The 1¾"-radius roundovers at the ends of the armrests and two of the legs allow the tabletop to pivot. Cut them with a jig saw.

Make sure the legs are square to the box frame, then fasten them together with glue and screws.

Directions: Table/chair

MAKE THE LEGS & ARMRESTS. The legs and armrests feature roundover cuts at the ends for increased stability and safety. Cut the legs (A) and armrests (F) to size from 1 × 4 oak. Use a compass to draw ¾"-radius curves on three corners of two of the legs, and at one end of the remaining two back legs. Cut the curves with a jig saw. On one corner of an armrest, draw a 1¾"-radius roundover and cut it with a jig saw. Use the roundover to trace identical curves at a corner of the other armrest, and at one square corner of the back legs. Cut the 1¾"-radius roundover in these parts **(photo A).** On the square end of each armrest, cut ¾"-radius curves on the corners.

BUILD THE BOX FRAME. Start by cutting the box sides (B), box ends (C) and box bottom (K) to size. Sand all parts with medium-grit sandpaper to smooth out any rough spots. Position the ends between the sides, then attach the sides and ends using glue and #6 × 1¼" wood screws, driven through the sides and into the ends. Be sure to drill evenly spaced pilot holes for the wood screws, counterbored to accept ⅜"-dia. wood plugs (throughout the project, counterbore all visible screw holes for ⅜"-dia. wood plugs). Next, use wood screws and glue to attach the bottom inside the ends and sides, flush with the bottom edges.

ATTACH THE BOX FRAME. The box frame fits between the legs, supporting the seat/shelf and creating storage. To attach it, first draw a reference line on one face of each leg, 10¾" up from the bottom. Clamp the armrests to the outside faces of the legs with the rounded corners up, keeping the top edges and ends flush. Make sure the 1¾" roundovers on the armrests

Fasten the seat to the hinge cleat with two brass butt hinges.

and the back legs are aligned. Position the box between the legs, so the top is flush with the reference lines on the legs. The box should be flush with the back edges of the rear legs, and ¾" in from the front edges of the front legs. Fasten the box between the legs with wood glue and #6 × 1¼" wood screws driven through counterbored pilot holes **(photo B).** Fasten the armrests to the outside faces of the legs with glue and #6 × 1" wood screws.

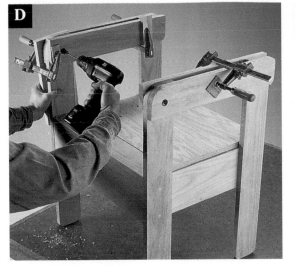

With a scrap block clamped to the outside of the
legs, drill guide holes for the dowel pivots.

The tabletop is attached to the table cleats with
brass corner brackets.

ATTACH THE SEAT. The seat
(or shelf) for the table/chair is
hinged to a 1 × 4 cleat that
mounts to the back of the box
frame. Start by cutting the
hinge cleat (D) and the seat
(E) to size. Cut strips of ¾" oak
veneer edge tape to fit all four
edges of the seat, then press
them in place with a household iron. After the tape cools,
trim off any excess with a sharp
utility knife, then sand the
edges smooth. Attach a pair of
3 × 1½" brass butt hinges to the
mating edges of the hinge cleat
and the seat board. Make sure
any overhang is equal on each
side. Install the hinges on the
seat, about 2" in from each
end, then fasten the seat to the
hinge cleat **(photo C).** Attach
the hinge cleat to the back
edge of the box frame with
glue and #6 × 2" wood screws.

MAKE THE TABLETOP. Start by
cutting the tabletop (H) and
table cleats (G) to size. Apply
oak veneer edge tape to all
four edges of the top. Use a
compass to draw a ¾"-radius
curve onto two of the corners
of each cleat, aligned on the
same edge. Cut the curves with

a jig saw. Next, you'll need to
drill guide holes for the dowel
pivots. Clamp the table cleats
to the inside faces of the legs,
so the top and front edges are
flush (also slip a scrap block
over the outside face of each
armrest before drilling). Mark
drilling points that are 1¾"
down from the top and 1¾" in
from the back end of each armrest. Drill ¾"-dia. guide holes
through the armrests, legs and
table cleats at the drilling
points, using a ¾" spade bit
(photo D). Also mark drilling
points for ⅜"-dia. guide holes
for the lock pins ⅞" up from the
bottom edges of the armrests
and ⅞" in from the inside edges
of the back legs. Drill the guide
holes for the lock pins with a ⅜"
spade bit. Cut the pivots (I) and
lock pins (J) from oak doweling and test the fit.

APPLY THE FINISH. Before attaching the tabletop, apply a
finish to the parts. We used
medium-oak wood stain with
two coats of polyurethane. Be
sure to glue wood plugs into all
counterbores and finish-sand
thoroughly before applying
the finish.

ATTACH THE TABLETOP.
Replace the table cleats next
to the legs and clamp in place
with ⅛"-thick spacers between
the table cleats and legs. Coat
the pivot pins lightly with glue
and drive them into the guide
holes to join the table cleats,
legs and armrests. Drill a pilot
hole for a 4d finish nail through
the back end of each armrest
and into the pivot, then drive a
finish nail to secure each pivot.
Apply glue to the tops of table
cleats, then center the tabletop
over the cleats so it overhangs
the legs by 3" at the front and
back, and 1½" at the sides.
Clamp the tabletop to the armrests, then fasten a 1¼ × 1¼"
brass corner brace at each
joint, about 1" in from the front
of each table cleat. Unclamp
the tabletop, then carefully tilt
it up so you have access to attach the rest of the corner
braces. Attach two more
braces, evenly spaced, to the
table cleats and the tabletop
(photo E). Lower the tabletop,
apply paste wax to the locking
pins, then drive the pins into
their guide holes to secure the
top in the down position.

Entry Valet

The friendly face of this valet hides the fact that it's a functional storage unit, with a drop-down bin and a covered scarf box.

CONSTRUCTION MATERIALS

Quantity	Lumber
1	1 × 12" × 6' pine
2	1 × 10" × 8' pine
1	1 × 6" × 6' pine
1	1 × 4" × 6' pine
1	1 × 3" × 6' pine
1	¾" × 6' pine stop molding
1	¼" × 4 × 4' plywood

This entry valet is designed to provide handy storage in one of the busiest areas of your house—the entryway. It is equipped with a spacious pivoting bin at the top, and a scarf storage box with a hinged lid that also functions as a shelf and a stretcher to give the valet added strength.

Because the entry is the first part of your house that most visitors will see, it is important that entry furnishings be pleasing to look at, as well as functional. For that reason, we used simple construction that is reminiscent of popular Shaker styling, and added decorative contours that give the valet a touch of Colonial style as well.

38

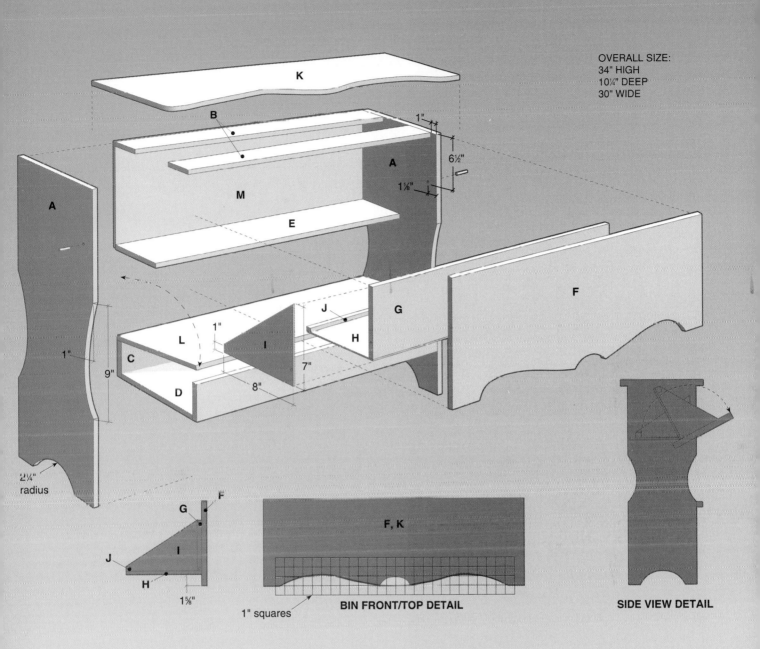

OVERALL SIZE:
34" HIGH
10¼" DEEP
30" WIDE

1"

6½"

1⅛"

A

K

B

M

E

A

F

G

H

J

I

L

C

D

1"

7"

8"

9"

1"

2¼"
radius

F

G

I

J

H

1⅝"

F, K

BIN FRONT/TOP DETAIL

1" squares

SIDE VIEW DETAIL

Cutting List

Key	Part	Dimension	Pcs.	Material
A	End	¾ × 9¼ × 33¼"	2	Pine
B	Top stretcher	¾ × 2½ × 28½"	2	Pine
C	Box side	¾ × 3½ × 28½"	2	Pine
D	Box bottom	¾ × 7¾ × 28½"	1	Pine
E	Bin stop	¾ × 5½ × 28½"	1	Pine
F	False front	¾ × 9¼ × 28¼"	1	Pine
G	Bin front	¾ × 5½ × 27⅝"	1	Pine

Cutting List

Key	Part	Dimension	Pcs.	Material
H	Bin bottom	¼ × 8 × 27⅝"	1	Plywood
I	Bin side	¼ × 7 × 8"	2	Plywood
J	Bin back lip	¾ × ¾ × 27⅝"	1	Stop molding
K	Top	¾ × 10¼ × 32"	1	Pine
L	Lid	¾ × 9½ × 28¼"	1	Pine
M	Valet back	¼ × 8 × 29½"	1	Plywood

Materials: Wood glue, 1" wire nails, #6 × 1¼" wood screws, ⅜" dowel (2), finishing materials, 2" butt hinges (2).

Note: Measurements reflect the actual size of dimensional lumber.

39

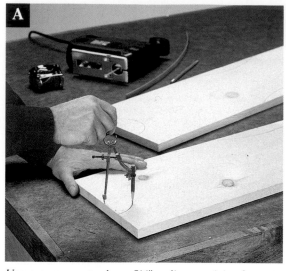

Use a compass to draw 2¼"-radius semicircular cutting lines on the bottoms of the end pieces.

Fasten the bin stop board between the end panels to complete the assembly of the basic valet framework.

Fasten the bin sides with wire nails and glue.

Directions: Entry Valet

CUT & CONTOUR THE END PIECES. The ends of the valet are made from pieces of 1 × 10 pine with curved contours cut at the sides and at the bottom of each panel. Cut the end panels (A) to size. To make the side cutouts, mark points at each side edge, 17⅜" from the bottom of each end. At the points, measure in 1" from the edge to mark the deepest point of each side cutout. Mark points 4½" above and below each mark at the side edges to mark the endpoints for the cutouts. Draw smooth, curved lines from endpoint to endpoint, through the centerpoints. To draw the lines, flex a ruler between endpoints as a guide, or make a cardboard template to trace the cutouts. Make the cutouts with a jig saw, then sand out any rough spots. To make the bottom cutouts, mark the center of each end panel on the bottom edge. Set a compass to 2¼" radius, and set the tip on a centerpoint. Draw a semicircular cutting line at the bottom of each panel **(photo A).** Make the cutouts and sand smooth.

ASSEMBLE THE FRAMEWORK. The contoured end pieces are fitted together with the scarf box (C, D), the top stretchers (B), and the bin stop (E) to make the general framework for the valet. Cut these pieces to size. Build the scarf box by fastening together the bottom and the sides with glue and #6 × 1¼" screws. Counterbore pilot holes to accept ⅜"-dia. wood plugs. Three or four evenly spaced screws driven through the box sides and into the edges of the box bottom are

plenty. Attach the box assembly to the inside faces of the end panels, so the box sides are flush with the front and back edges of the end panels. The bottom of the box should be 7¼" up from the bottoms of the end panels. Attach the top stretchers between the end panels, flat face up, using glue and counterbored screws. One stretcher should be flush with the back and top edges of the end panels, and the other should be flush with the tops, but recessed 1" from the front edges (see *Diagram*, page 39). Finally, install the bin stop between the end panels, 7½" down from the tops of the panels, and flush with the back edges **(photo B).**

BUILD THE BIN. The dropdown bin pivots on dowels to open up for storage. Cut the bin front (G) and the bin bottom (H). Attach the bin bottom to the bin front with glue and 1" wire nails driven up through the bottom and into the front piece. Next, cut the triangular bin sides (I) (see *Diagram*, page 39). Attach the sides to the bottom/front assembly with

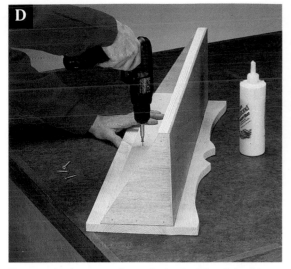

Drive wood screws through the inside of the bin and into the back of the false front.

Clamp the bin to the valet framework, then drill dowel holes through the sides and into the bin.

glue and wire nails **(photo C).** Cut a piece of ¾ × ¾" pine stop molding to length to make the bin back lip (J). Glue the lip to the bin bottom so the ends fit between the bin sides.

MAKE & ATTACH THE FALSE FRONT FOR THE BIN. The false front (F) is attached to the front of the bin to create a decorative apron for the valet. To make the false front, cut a piece of 1 × 10 pine to size, then plot out a grid with 1" squares on the face of the board. Using the pattern on page 39 as a guide, draw the cutout shape onto the false front, and cut out with a jig saw. Sand smooth. Draw a reference line on the inside face of the false front, 1⅝" up from the bottom edge. Attach the false front to the bin front so the bin rides on the reference line. Use glue and #6 × 1¼" wood screws driven through the bin, and into the false front **(photo D).**

INSTALL THE BIN. Set the completed bin onto the bin stop board between the end panels so it is flush against the outside top stretcher and the bin stop.

Use spacer blocks and C-clamps to hold the bin in place. Mount a portable drill stand to your portable drill, and drill a ⅜"-dia. × 1⅝"-deep hole through each end panel and into the sides of the bin **(photo E).** The center-points of the holes should be 6½" down from the tops of the end panels, and 1⅛" in from the front edges. Cut two 1½"-long pieces from a ⅜"-dia. dowel, and insert them in the holes. Remove the C-clamps.

APPLY THE FINISHING TOUCHES. With the bin still pinned in place, cut the valet top (K) to size, then make the decorative cutout on the front edge using the same pattern and techniques used for the bin false front (the valet top does not have the small scallop in the center that is cut into the false front). Also cut the scarf box lid (L). Remove the bin, finish-sand all surfaces, and apply your finish of choice. We used orange shellac (a traditional finishing product for pine). Once the parts are finished, attach the lid to the box with 2" butt hinges at the back of the lid, and attach the valet

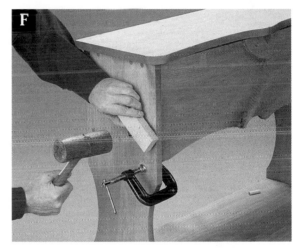

Using a wood block to prevent splitting, drive dowels into the dowel holes to serve as pivots.

top to the end panels with glue and wood screws counterbored for wood plugs. Before installing the bin, squirt wood glue into the dowel holes in the bin. Replace the bin, and drive the dowels into the dowel holes. Use a wood block to prevent splitting the dowels **(photo F).** After the glue sets, sand the dowels flush with the sides of the valet, and stain to match the rest of the wood. Cut a back (M) for the valet and tack it to the back edges of the end panels and to the top stretcher, using wire nails.

Bread Box

Reduce the clutter on your countertop and add some country charm to your kitchen with this combination bread box and toaster garage.

CONSTRUCTION MATERIALS

Quantity	Lumber
1	1 × 8" × 8' oak
1	1 × 14 to16" × 4' oak panel

Add a down-home feeling to your kitchen with this uniquely styled combination bread box and toaster garage. Reminiscent of antique bread boxes, our design is updated to include a storage space for your toaster and a removable cutting board. The cutting board fits against the front of the bread box, concealing the toaster, and is held in place by the closed lid. Position the bread box close to an electrical outlet and pull the toaster out to use it, then tuck it back inside the bread box when you're finished. The cutting board works well as a preparation area and also as a crumb catcher to help keep cleanup time to a minimum.

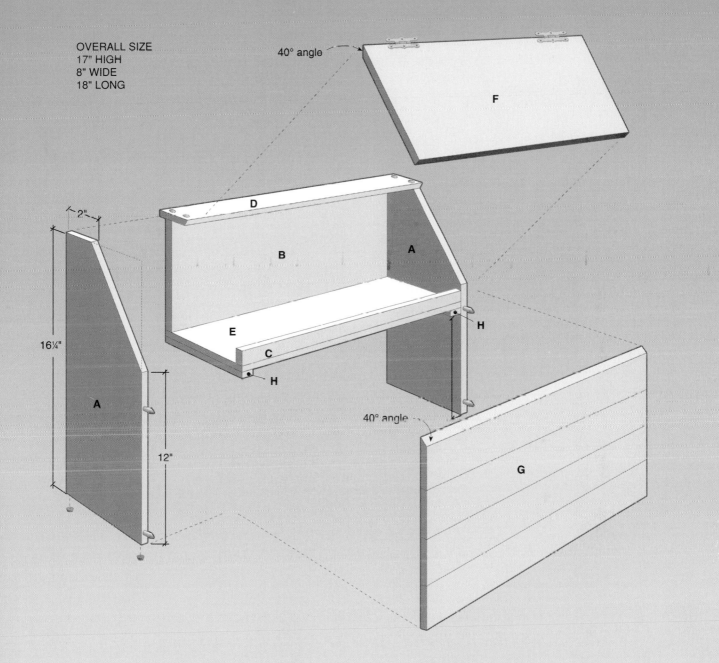

OVERALL SIZE
17" HIGH
8" WIDE
18" LONG

40° angle

F

2"

D

B

A

16¼"

A

E

C

H

12"

H

40° angle

G

Cutting List				
Key	**Part**	**Dimension**	**Pcs.**	**Material**
A	Side	¾ × 7¼ × 16¼"	2	Oak
B	Back	¾ × 7¼ × 16½"	1	Oak
C	Front lip	¾ × 1½ × 16½"	1	Oak
D	Top	¾ × 2¼ × 18"	1	Oak

Cutting List				
Key	**Part**	**Dimension**	**Pcs.**	**Material**
E	Bread shelf	¾ × 7¼ × 16½"	1	Oak
F	Lid	¾ × 9 × 18"	1	Oak
G	Cutting board	¾ × 12 × 18"	1	Oak
H	Cleat	¾ × 1 × 7¼"	2	Oak

Materials: Wood glue, #6 x 1¼" brass wood screws, (4) ⅜"-dia. wood table pins, 4 rubber glide feet.

Specialty items: Hand plane, preglued oak panels.

Note: Measurements reflect the actual size of dimensional lumber.

Use a circular saw to trim off corners at the tops of both side pieces.

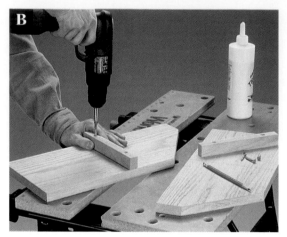

Fasten the cleats for the bread shelf to the box sides, using wood glue and brass screws.

Directions: Bread Box

MAKE THE SIDES. The sides of the bread box are simple rectangles with one corner removed to create a surface for the lid that slopes down from back to front. Start by cutting the sides (A) from 1 × 8 oak. Mark the endpoints for the tapered trim lines by measuring in 2" from a corner along the top edge of each side, then measuring down 12" from the same corner (see *Diagram*, page 43). Connect the endpoints, then cut at the line with a circular saw **(photo A).** Sand all edges and surfaces smooth. Cut the shelf cleats (H). On the inside surfaces of the sides, measure down 8" from the tops and draw a line. Place the top edge of the cleats along the line, and drill countersunk pilot holes through the cleats into the sides. Fasten the cleats to the sides with glue and #6 × 1¼" wood screws **(photo B).**

ASSEMBLE THE BOX. The sides, back, front and bread shelf form the basic box construction. Cut the bread shelf (E). Using glue and screws, fasten the bread shelf between the sides so it rests on the side

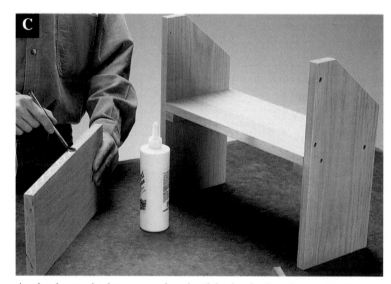

Apply glue to the bottom and ends of the back, then fasten it to the box sides with brass wood screws.

cleats. Cut the back (B), and attach it between the sides, with its bottom edge resting on the bread shelf **(photo C).** Make sure the back is flush with the back edges of the sides. Use glue and screws driven through the sides and into the ends of the back. Counterbore the pilot holes to accept oak plugs (usually ⅜"-dia.). Cut the front lip (C), and set it on the bread shelf, between the sides and flush with the front edge of the shelf. Drill counterbored pilot holes through the sides into the front lip and fasten in place with wood glue and screws.

MAKE THE LID & CUTTING BOARD. The lid and cutting board are wider than standard oak board widths. To make these parts, you can either edge-glue several strips of oak together (a relatively difficult operation that requires a lot of belt-sander work), or you can purchase preglued oak panels. Preglued panels are sold in several widths, from 14 to 24". They are solid hardwood (as opposed to plywood) so they are still good materials to use for cutting-board projects. Cut the lid (F) and cutting board (G) to length from an oak

44

Cut 40° bevels on one edge of the lid, the top and the cutting board using a circular saw.

Drill ⅜"-dia. holes in the front edges of the sides for the table pins that hold the cutting board in place.

panel. The top (D) is only 2¼" wide when finished, but the bevel cut on the front edge will be much easier to make on a wider board, so you will be better off cutting it from a piece of 1 × 6 or 1 × 8. The top edge of the cutting board, the front edge of the top and the back edge of the lid are cut with bevels that match the slope of the sides. Set your circular saw to make a 40° bevel cut. Make a test cut on a piece of scrap wood first to make sure the angle matches the side profile, then use a straightedge guide to bevel-cut the back edge of the lid **(photo D).** Also bevel-cut the top edge of the cutting board and the front edge of the top. When cut, the taller side of the lid should measure 9", and the taller side of the cutting board should be 12".

ATTACH THE TOP, LID & CUTTING BOARD. The top strip is attached to the tops of the side and the back with screws. It supports the lid, which is attached to it with hinges. The cutting board is fitted over four table pins that are mounted in the front edges of the sides. When the lid is closed, it holds the cutting board in place.

Position the top on the side panels, flush with the outside surfaces of the sides. Drill counterbored pilot holes through the top into the top edges of the sides, and fasten with glue and #6 × 1¼" brass wood screws. Drill a pair of ⅜"-dia. holes in the front edge of each side 1" and 8" up from the bottom. The holes should be deep enough so ⅜" of the table pins will protrude out when the pins are inserted **(photo E).** Apply glue to the blunt ends of the table pins and tap them into the holes with a wood or rubber mallet. Attach brass butt hinges to the lid, 2½" in from

each end, then attach the top to the hinges. Rub chalk on the points of the table pins and place the cutting board in position against the pins to mark the hole locations **(photo F).** Drill ⅜"-dia. × ⅜"-deep holes in the cutting board at the corresponding locations.

APPLY FINISHING TOUCHES. Apply glue and insert button plugs in the screw hole counterbores. Finish-sand the entire bread box. Apply several coats of salad bowl oil for a nontoxic protective finish. Fasten rubber glide feet to the four bottom corners of the bread box.

Rub chalk on the points of the table pins and press the cutting board in position against the pins to mark drilling locations on the cutting board.

Kitchen Island

Our stand-alone cabinet and countertop island expands the versatility of any kitchen.

CONSTRUCTION MATERIALS

Quantity	Lumber
7	⅝" × 2 × 4' pine panel
4	1 × 2" × 8' pine
1	1 × 4" × 4' pine
1	2 × 8" × 2' pine
4	¾ × ¾" × 8' pine stop molding
1	¾" × 4 × 4' particleboard
1	¼" × 4 × 4' tileboard

This project is a great-looking alternative to more expensive custom cabinetry, and every bit as useful. The kitchen island gives you additional space for preparing food, as well as a convenient spot to enjoy a light snack or a quick meal. The ends, back panels and shelves are constructed from edge-glued ponderosa pine, a convenient building material that provides a distinctively appealing pattern for cabinetry. The front of the island sports a finished face frame and features adjustable shelving for dishes or other cooking utensils. The countertop has an 8" overhang and provides room for two to sit comfortably.

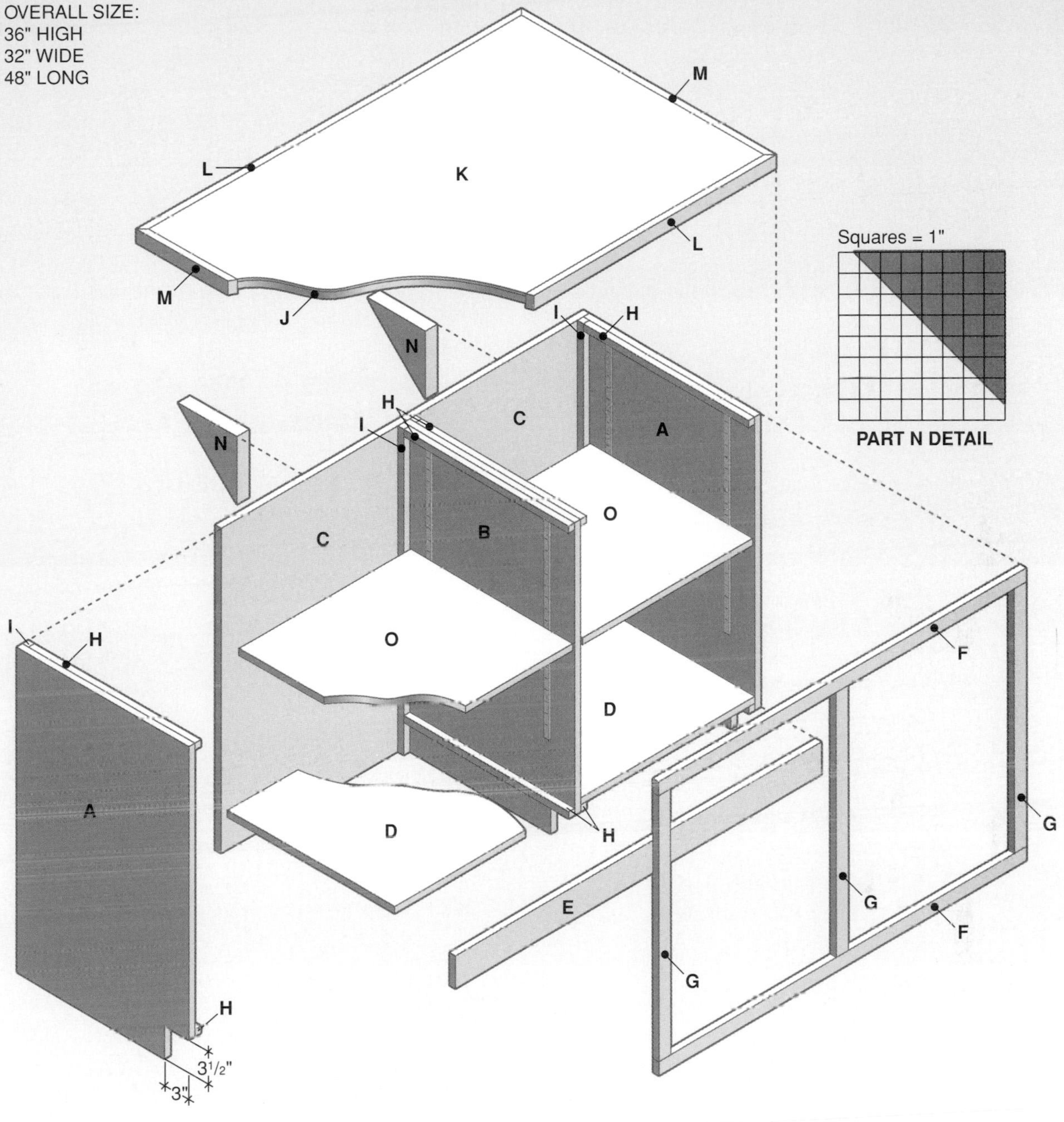
OVERALL SIZE:
36" HIGH
32" WIDE
48" LONG
M
L
K
L
M
J
N
I
H
N
H
I
C
A
O
C
B
I
H
O
D
A
D
H
F
G
E
G
F
G
H
3½"
3"
Squares = 1"
PART N DETAIL

Cutting List				
Key	**Part**	**Dimension**	**Pcs.**	**Material**
A	End	⅝ × 21½ × 35"	2	Pine panel
B	Divider	⅝ × 21½ × 35"	1	Pine panel
C	Back	⅝ × 22⅛ × 35"	2	Pine panel
D	Bottom	⅝ × 21⅛ × 21½"	2	Pine panel
E	Toe board	¾ × 3½ × 44¼"	1	Pine
F	Rail	¾ × 1½ × 44¼"	2	Pine
G	Stile	¾ × 1½ × 28½"	3	Pine
H	Horiz. cleat	¾ × ¾ × 20¾"	8	Molding

Cutting List				
Key	**Part**	**Dimension**	**Pcs.**	**Material**
I	Vert. cleat	¾ × ¾ × 35"	4	Molding
J	Substrate	¾ × 30½ × 46½"	1	Particleboard
K	Top	¼ × 30½ × 46½"	1	Tileboard
L	Long edge	¾ × 1½ × 48"	2	Pine
M	Short edge	¾ × 1½ × 32"	2	Pine
N	Support	1½ × 7¼ × 7¼"	2	Pine
O	Shelf	⅝ × 20½ × 20½"	2	Pine panel

Materials: Wood glue, #6 wood screws (1", 1¼", 1½"), ½" tacks, 4d finish nails, 24" shelf standards (8), shelf standard supports, contact cement, finishing materials.

Cut the toe board notches into the ends and divider using a jig saw.

Gang the cleats together while drilling countersunk pilot holes.

Directions: Kitchen Island

CUT THE ENDS AND DIVIDER. Cut the ends (A) and divider (B) to size from pine panels, using a circular saw. Measure and mark the 3"-wide × 3½"-tall toe board notches on the lower front corners of all three pieces using a combination square (see *Diagram*). This notch and the toe board provide a *kick space*, allowing you to

approach a cabinet without stubbing your toes against the bottom. Clamp each piece to your worksurface, and cut out the toe board notches using a jig saw **(photo A)**.

PREPARE THE CLEATS. The cleats reinforce the internal joints of the cabinet. Countersunk pilot holes are drilled through each cleat in two directions, and are offset so the screws won't hit one another.

Cut the horizontal cleats (H) and the vertical cleats (I) to length from ¾ × ¾" stop molding. Clamp the vertical cleats together so the ends are flush, and mark four pilot hole locations along the length of each cleat (see *Detail* for pilot hole locations). Place the clamped cleats on a piece of scrap plywood, and drill countersunk pilot holes at each marked location. Remove the clamps and give each cleat a quarter turn. Reclamp the cleats, then mark and drill the second set of offset pilot holes. Repeat the process for the horizontal cleats, drilling three holes through one edge of each cleat and two offset holes through an adjacent edge **(photo B)**.

ASSEMBLE THE ENDS AND DIVIDER. Align a vertical cleat along the inside back edge of

PARTS H AND I DETAIL

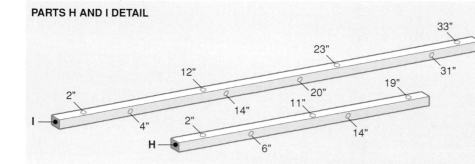

Center a marked template between the cleats to uniformly attach the shelf standards.

Clamp the back to the divider along the centerline, and adjust when attaching to the end.

one of the ends. Align the pilot holes so the back can be attached through the offset holes. Apply glue and fasten the cleat to the end with countersunk 1" screws. Attach vertical cleats to the inside face of the other end, and to both back edges of the divider. Attach the horizontal cleats to the ends and divider, using glue and 1" screws.

ATTACH THE SHELF STANDARDS. The shelf standards are positioned on the ends and divider with the aid of a simple template. Cut a 15 × 30" template from scrap particleboard or heavy-stock cardboard. Make sure the standards are properly aligned in the same direction so the holes for the supports uniformly line up. Place the template on the lower horizontal cleat, and cen-

ter the template between the vertical cleat and the front edge. Measure 2" up from the bottom edge along each side of the template and make a reference mark. Place a standard against each edge of the template and adjust so the bottom of the standard is on the 2" mark. Nail the standards in place with ½" tacks. Do the same on the other end, and on

both faces of the divider **(photo C).**

ASSEMBLE THE CABINET. Cut the backs (C), bottoms (D) and toe board (E) to size, and sand the edges smooth. Cut ¾ × ¾" notches in the back corners of each bottom to accommodate the vertical cleats.

Stand one end and the divider upright on their front edges. Then position a bottom

TIP

The back, end, divider, bottom and shelf pieces used in this project are constructed from ⅝" edge-glued ponderosa pine panels, available at most building centers. This material, available in varying dimensions and thicknesses, is manufactured from small-width pine glued together under pressure. The result is a strong material that is slightly thinner than standard dimensional plywood. It features a distinctive paneled appearance, and since it is made entirely of one type of wood, exposed edges do not require veneer.

E

F

Arrange the bottom rail so the corners and edges are flush, and attach to the divider and ends with glue and 4d finish nails.

Sand the rails after the stiles to avoid cross-sanding marks on the rails.

piece against the lower horizontal cleats. Use bar clamps to hold the assembly in place, and attach the bottom with glue and 1" screws driven through the pilot holes in each cleat. Position the remaining bottom and end in place, and attach the bottom to the cleats.

Attach the back pieces one at a time, using glue and 1" screws driven through the vertical cleats inside the cabinet. Make sure each back piece is aligned with its inside edge flush against a marked reference centerline on the divider. Check frequently for square, and use pipe clamps to hold the pieces in position as you attach them **(photo D).**

Carefully turn the assembly over, and fasten the toe board in place with glue and 4d finish nails.

ASSEMBLE THE FACE FRAME. Cut the rails (F) and stiles (G) to size, and sand them smooth. Position the top rail so the top edges and corners are flush, and attach with glue and finish nails. Attach the stiles so the outside edges are flush with the end faces and centered on the divider. Finally, attach the bottom rail **(photo E).** Reinforce the joints by drilling pilot holes through the rails into the ends of each stile and securing with 4d finish nails. Use an orbital sander to smooth the face frame and the joints between

stiles and rails. By sanding the stiles before the rails, you can avoid cross-sanding marks at the joints **(photo F).**

BUILD THE COUNTERTOP. Cut the substrate (J), top (K), long edges (L) and short edges (M) to size. Make sure the top fits perfectly over the substrate, and trim if necessary. Miter-cut the ends of the long edges and short edges at 45° angles to fit around the countertop.

Apply contact cement to the substrate, and clamp the top in place, using scrap wood under the clamps to distribute pressure and ensure even contact with the cement **(photo G).**

When dry, unclamp and flip the assembly on its top. Arrange

Clamping scrap boards to the tileboard helps distribute pressure and evens contact.

Attach the supports to the back from inside the cabinet using glue and screws.

the long and short edges around the countertop, so the top surface will be flush with the tops of the edge pieces. Glue and clamp the edges in place. Drill pilot holes and drive 4d finish nails through the edges into the substrate.

ATTACH THE COUNTERTOP AND SHELVES. Cut the shelves (O) from pine panels. Cut the supports (N) from 2 × 8 dimensional pine. (A single 7¼ × 7¼" piece cut diagonally will create these supports.) Break the cut corners at the ends of each diagonal, using a jig saw or a sander. This softens the profile of the supports and reduces the chance of snagged clothing under the countertop.

To attach the supports, mark a line on the top edge of the back, 11" in from each end. Position the supports so they are centered on the lines. Then drill pilot holes through the back and attach the supports with glue and 1½" screws driven from the inside of the cabinet **(photo H).**

Center the countertop from side to side on the cabinet with a 1" overhang on the front. Attach with glue and 1¼" screws driven up through the top horizontal cleats. Insert supports into the shelf standards at the desired height, and install the shelves inside the cabinet with the grain running left to right.

APPLY FINISHING TOUCHES. Recess all visible nail heads with a nail set, and fill the holes with putty. Sand all surfaces, outer edges and corners smooth. Finish the kitchen island with a light stain (we used a traditional American pine finish), and apply a nontoxic topcoat.

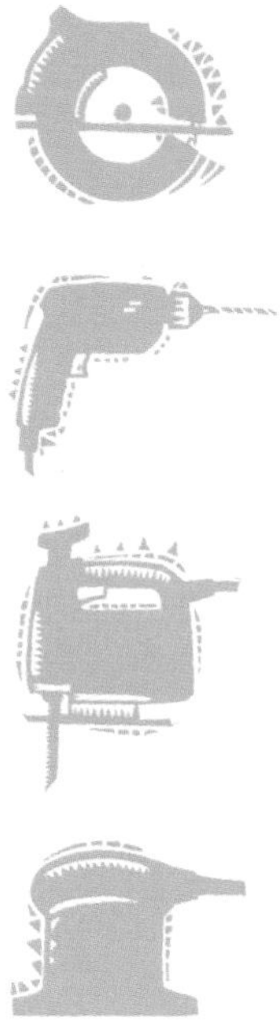

Pop-up Wine Bar

*Flip up the tabletop and slide out the oak plywood stools to enjoy a
a glass or two of your favorite wine vintage in an intimate setting.*

CONSTRUCTION MATERIALS

Quantity	Lumber
2	¾" × 4 × 8' oak plywood
1	2 × 2" × 4' oak
1	1 × 2" × 8' oak
1	¾ × ¾" × 4' oak quarter-round molding

Special wines deserve a special environment to be properly shared with a friend. With this pop-up wine bar, you can create an instant cafe setting, complete with stools and a wine rack. When the wine bar is not in use, the stools store neatly inside the cabinet opening, and the bar folds back down so the whole unit is about the size of a small bookcase. The storage rack at the side is easily accessible at all times, and the cabinet top makes a handy surface for temporary storage.

Made of edge-banded oak plywood and solid oak trim boards, the wine bar is a sturdy piece of furniture that knows how to conquer space.

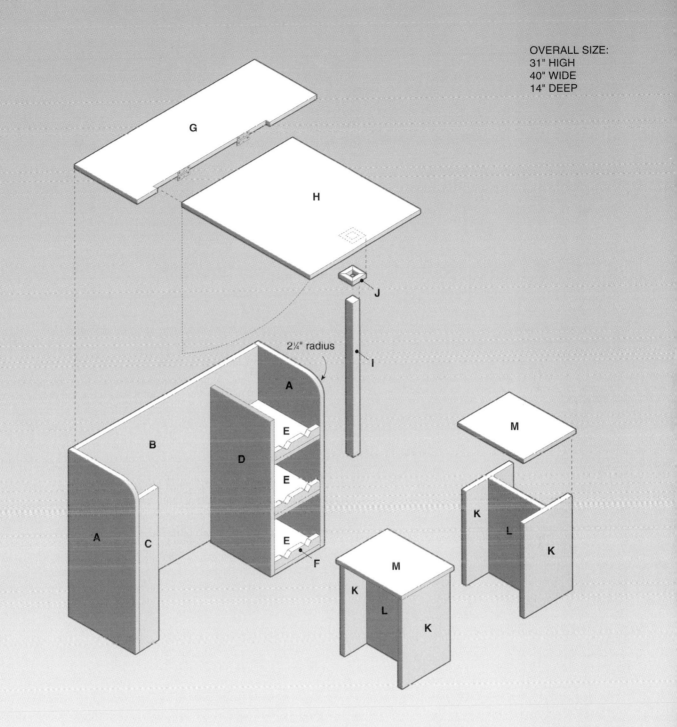

OVERALL SIZE:
31" HIGH
40" WIDE
14" DEEP

2¼" radius

G

H

J

I

A

E

B

D

E

A

C

E

F

M

K

L

K

M

K

L

K

Cutting List

Key	Part	Dimension	Pcs.	Material
A	Side panel	¾ × 14 × 31"	2	Oak Plywood
B	Back panel	¾ × 38½ × 31"	1	Oak Plywood
C	Filler strip	¾ × 4¼ × 28¼"	1	Oak Plywood
D	Center panel	¾ × 13 × 28¼"	1	Oak Plywood
E	Shelf	¾ × 9½ × 13"	3	Oak Plywood
F	Bottle support	¾ × 1½ × 9½"	3	Oak
G	Top panel	¾ × 13 × 38½"	1	Oak

Cutting List

Key	Part	Dimension	Pcs.	Material
H	Tabletop	¾ × 23⅞ × 27"	1	Oak Plywood
I	Leg	1½ × 1½ × 28¼"	1	Oak
J	Leg molding	¾ × ¾ × 3"	4	Oak Molding
K	Stool side	¾ × 10 × 17¼"	4	Oak Plywood
L	Stool center	¾ × 9½ × 17¼"	2	Oak Plywood
M	Stool seat	¾ × 11 × 12"	2	Oak Plywood

Materials: Wood glue, #6 × 1⅝" wood screws, ⅜"-dia. oak plugs, finishing materials, 3d & 6d finish nails, oak tape (50').

Note: Measurements reflect the actual thickness of dimensional lumber.

Cut the curves on the top front corners of the side panels with a jig saw.

Use a household iron to press veneer edge tape onto the plywood edges—the heat activates the self-adhesive backing.

Carefully trim off any excess veneer tape from the top and bottom, using a sharp utility knife.

Directions: Pop-up Wine Bar

MAKE THE CABINET PANELS. The back and side cabinet panels form the main shell of the wine bar. We made them from ¾" oak plywood, with veneer edge tape to conceal the edges of the boards. The top, front edges of the side panels are rounded over, helping to create a three-sided splashboard that frames the tabletop. Cut the side panels (A) and back panel (B) to size, using a circular saw and straightedge cutting guide. Next, lay out the curved portions at the top front corners of the side panels with a compass set to form a curve with a 2¼" radius. Cut the curves with a jig saw **(photo A),** then sand the edges and surfaces of the panels with medium-grit sandpaper to smooth out any rough spots and saw marks. Clean the top of the back panel and the tops and sides of the side panels thoroughly, then cut strips of self-adhesive oak veneer edge tape to fit—use one strip only for each side to follow the curves. Place a strip over each edge, and set each strip in place by pressing it with a household iron set to low-to-medium heat **(photo B).** The heat activates the adhesive. When the adhesive has cooled and set, trim the edges of the strips with a sharp utility knife **(photo C),** then sand the edges and corners with medium-grit sandpaper to remove any irregularities. Clamp the side panels to the back panel so the sides cover the side edges of the back panel, and the bottoms

are flush. Drill pilot holes for #6 × 1⅝" wood screws at 6 to 8" intervals in the side panels, then counterbore the pilot holes for ⅜"-dia. wood plugs. Unclamp the parts, glue the edges and clamp them back together. Drive 1⅝" wood screws through the pilot holes to reinforce the joints.

INSTALL THE SHELF UNIT. The shelf unit fits on the right side of the cabinet to create storage space for six wine bottles. The shelves that support the wine bottles are spaced about 10" apart for accessibility. If your wine collection consists of more than a half-dozen bottles, you can easily refigure the shelf spacing and add another shelf. A center plywood panel supports the shelves on the left side. Cut the center panel (D) and the shelves (E) to size. Apply veneer edge tape to the front edges of all parts. Then, stand the side panels and back panel assembly upright and fasten the bottom shelf at the bottom of the corner created by the right side panel and the back panel. Use glue and wood screws driven through counter-

Rest the shelves on plywood spacers to make it easier for you to install the shelves, and to ensure that the spacing is accurate.

bored pilot holes. Next, fasten the center panel with glue and screws driven through the center panel and into the left edge of the bottom shelf. Also drive screws through the back panel and into the back edge of the center panel, making sure the distance between the center panel and the left side panel is the same at the top and bottom. To make sure the upper shelves are spaced correctly, cut two 8⅝"-long spacers from scrap plywood and place them on the bottom shelf. Set the middle shelf on top of the spacers so the front edge is flush with the fronts of the side and center panels. Fasten the shelf with glue and screws (make sure to counterbore all pilot holes). Then set the spacers on the middle shelf, and fasten the top shelf in place **(photo D)**.

INSTALL THE BOTTLE SUPPORTS. The three shelves are trimmed in front with strips of 1 × 2 that feature pairs of V-shaped cutouts to support the necks of wine bottles. Cut the bottle supports (F) to length from 1 × 2 oak. Lay out the V-shaped cutouts for the bottle necks by measuring ¾" up from the bottom edge and 2½" in from each end and placing a mark. Using a combination square, mark a 45° angle in both directions from the marks to make the cutting lines for the cutouts **(photo E)**. Cut out the V-shapes using a jig saw. Sand the edges smooth. Fasten the bottle supports to the tops of the shelves so they are flush with the front shelf edges. Use glue and 6d finish nails (drill pilot holes) driven through the shelves and into the bottoms of the supports. Also drive a nail though the side panel and center panel, and into each end of each support.

ATTACH THE FILLER STRIP & TOP PANEL. Cut the filler strip (C) and top panel (G) to size.

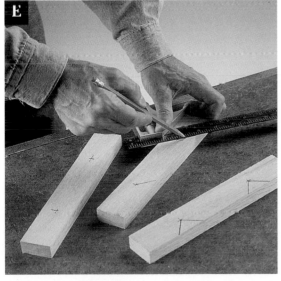

Use a combination square to lay out the V-shaped cutouts for the bottle necks.

The tabletop fits into a notch that is cut into the top panel with a jig saw—cut as straight as you can to make a clean joint.

The filler strip is installed on the left side of the cabinet to frame the cabinet opening and provide extra support for the tabletop. The top panel has a ¾" deep notch cut into the front edge to make a recess for hinging the tabletop. Lay out the notch on the top panel so it is ¾" deep, starting 10¼" from the right end and 4¼" from the left end. Cut the notch with a jig saw **(photo F),** using a straight-edge guide clamped to the board if you don't have a lot of experience cutting long lines with a jig saw. Smooth out the notch with medium-grit sandpaper. Apply veneer edge tape to the front edge and all three sides of the notch in the top panel, and apply tape to one of the long edges of the filler strip. Fasten the filler strip to the inside of the left cabinet side, flush with the bottom and ¼" back from the front edge. Use glue and #6 × 1⅝" wood screws driven through counterbored pilot holes. Then, install the top panel so it rests on the filler strip and the center panel, and the back edge is flush with the back panel (the front edge should also be flush with the fronts of the filler strip and the center panel). Use glue and counterbored screws, spaced at 8" intervals, to fasten the top panel.

MAKE THE TABLETOP. The tabletop is simply a rectangular piece of plywood with oak quarter-round molding fastened to the underside to hold the

The top of the table leg fits into a square pocket created by pieces of quarter-round molding attached to the underside of the tabletop.

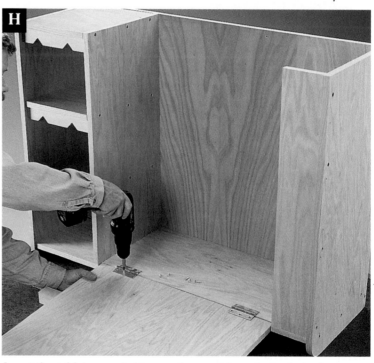

Invert the tabletop and side panel assembly and attach the butt hinges to the top panel, then fasten the tabletop to the hinges.

2 × 2 oak leg when the table is in use. Start by cutting the tabletop (H) to size from ¾"-thick oak plywood. Sand the edges and surfaces of the table top, then apply veneer edge tape to the edges of the tabletop. Sand the edges and surfaces smooth. Next, cut the leg (I) to length from 2 × 2 oak. Flip the tabletop upside down

and mark the leg pocket position by drawing a 1½" square that is 2" in from the front end and 11⅛" in from each side. Cut the leg molding (J) strips to frame the square and form a pocket to hold the leg. Miter the ends of the strips to make mitered joints at the corners of

Fasten the stool seat to the stool sides and stool centers with counterbored wood screws and glue.

APPLY FINISHING TOUCHES. Glue ⅜"-dia. oak wood plugs into all the screw hole counterbores, then sand the plugs flush with the surrounding wood. Drive the nail heads in the bottle supports below the surface, using a nail set. Sand all the wood surfaces and the edges of the wine table and stools with medium-grit sandpaper, then finish-sand the surfaces with fine-grit sandpaper. Wipe the wood clean with a rag dipped in mineral spirits, then apply a coat of sanding sealer and let it dry thoroughly. The sanding sealer helps the porous oak veneer layer absorb finish materials more evenly. Be sure to follow the manufacturer's directions and precautions when using any finishing material. After the sanding sealer has dried, using extra-fine sandpaper to lightly sand the sealed surfaces to remove any rough areas. Apply wood stain to the sealed surfaces with a paint brush or rag—a medium or darker-tone stain usually looks better with plywood than lighter stains. Let the stain dry completely, then apply two light coats of water-based polyurethane to the entire project. Add an extra coat or two to the surface of the tabletop.

the pocket (using a scrap of 2 × 2 as a gauge for the 1½" square will help quite a bit here). Fasten the molding around the square on the table-top with glue and 3d finish nails **(photo G).** Test-fit the leg in the pocket to be assured of a proper fit.

INSTALL THE TABLETOP. Set the cabinet upside down on a flat worksurface. Then, set the tabletop upside down on two pieces of scrap 2 × 2 and position the tabletop against the notch in the top panel. Attach a pair of 2½" butt hinges to the front edge of the top panel, then fasten the hinges to the tabletop **(photo H).**

BUILD THE STOOLS. The simple, four-board stools are constructed easily from oak plywood panels. They are sized to be housed for storage inside the opening in the cabinet part of the pop-up wine bar. Begin the stool construction by cutting the stool sides (K), stool centers (L) and stool seats (M) to size from ¾"-thick oak plywood. Apply wood veneer edge tape to the side edges of the stool sides and the perimeter edges of the stool seats. Trim the edge tape with a sharp utility knife and sand the edges and surfaces of the components with medium-grit sandpaper. Position the stool centers between the stool sides, centered on each stool side, then fasten the parts with counterbored #6 × 1⅝" wood screws and glue. Fasten the stool seat to the stool sides and stool centers with counterbored wood screws and glue **(photo I).**

TIP

Make sure the grain patterns run in the same direction when building with plywood. Even better-quality sheet goods, like oak plywood, tend to have very pronounced grain patterns, especially when you stain the wood. Having even one part in your project with grain running perpendicular to the other parts creates a very disappointing visual effect. Keep grain patterns in mind if you are making a sketch of how to cut the plywood sheets for most efficient use.

Covered Sandbox

The cedar canopy provides shelter from rain and sun when raised,
and keeps out pests and debris when lowered.

CONSTRUCTION MATERIALS

Quantity	Lumber
1	1 × 2" × 4' cedar
2	1 × 6" × 10' cedar
4	2 × 2" × 8' cedar
4	2 × 4" × 8' cedar
1	2 × 6" × 8' cedar
3	2 × 8" × 8' cedar
1	⅜" × 4' × 8' cedar plywood

Sandboxes are a backyard favorite for youngsters everywhere, but they do have a few natural enemies: rain, fallen leaves, backyard debris, and even neighborhood cats can make any sandbox uninviting. That's why we designed this roomy cedar sandbox with a sturdy cover that protects against these ene- mies when it is lowered over the top of the box. We took that good idea one step further by creating the cover so it can be supported by removable corner posts to do double duty as a sun and rain shelter when the sandbox is being used. When the cover is lowered, the posts can be stored neatly inside the sandbox.

OVERALL SIZE:
50⅞" HIGH
49½" WIDE
49½" LONG

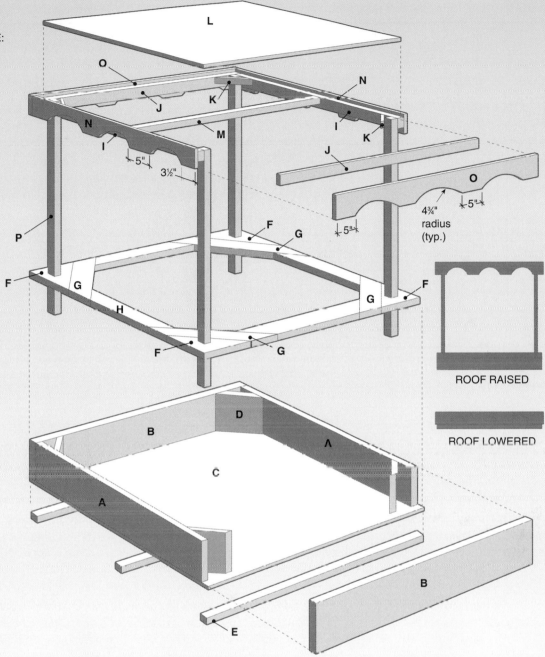

ROOF RAISED

ROOF LOWERED

Cutting List

Key	Part	Dimension	Pcs.	Material
A	End rail	1½ × 7¼ × 45"	2	Cedar
B	Side rail	1½ × 7¼ × 48"	2	Cedar
C	Bottom panel	⅜ × 48 × 48"	1	Plywood
D	Post cleat	1½ × 7¼ × 7"	4	Cedar
E	Base cleat	1½ × 1½ × 48"	3	Cedar
F	Corner brace	1½ × 7¼ × 7¼"	4	Cedar
G	Corner seat	1½ × 5½ × 21¼"	4	Cedar
H	Ledge	1½ × 3½ × 25"	4	Cedar

Cutting List

Key	Part	Dimension	Pcs.	Material
I	End frame	1½ × 3½ × 45"	2	Cedar
J	Side frame	1½ × 3½ × 48"	2	Cedar
K	Top post cleat	¾ × 1½ × 5⅝"	4	Cedar
L	Top panel	⅜ × 48 × 48"	1	Plywood
M	Stringer	1½ × 1½ × 45"	1	Cedar
N	End apron	¾ × 5½ × 40"	2	Cedar
O	Side apron	¾ × 5½ × 49½"	2	Cedar
P	Post	1½ × 1½ × 48"	4	Cedar

Materials: Moisture-resistant wood glue, galvanized deck screws (1¼", 3"), 8d galvanized finish nails.

Note: Measurements reflect the actual size of dimensional lumber.

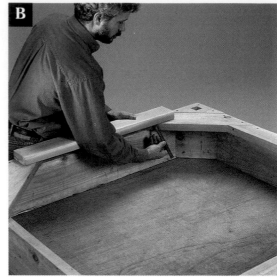

Install the corner braces to create post standards and to strengthen the corners of the sandbox.

Lay the ledges between the corners and trace cutting lines where they meet the corner seats.

Directions: Covered Sandbox

BUILD THE SANDBOX FRAME. The sandbox frame is a simple box frame made from 2 × 8 cedar. Cut the end rails (A) and side rails (B) to length. Lay the rails on edge on a flat worksurface. Place the end rails between the side rails flush with the ends of the side rails to form a square frame. Drill three evenly spaced pilot holes for 3" deck screws at each joint, drilling through the side rails and into the end of the end rails (you may want to clamp the pieces together first). Countersink the pilot holes slightly so the screw heads will be recessed. Apply moisture-resistant glue to the boards at each joint, then drive a 3" deck screw at each pilot hole.

ATTACH THE BASE. The sandbox has a cedar plywood base that rests on three 2 × 2 cedar slats to minimize ground contact with the sandbox. Cut a 4 × 8 sheet of ⅜"-thick textured cedar siding (a plywood product) in half to make the bottom

panel (C). Cut carefully so you can use the other half of the sheet for the cover. Fasten the bottom panel, smooth surface up, to the bottom edges of the sandbox frame pieces with moisture-resistant glue and 1¼" deck screws. Cut the 2 × 2 base cleats (E), and fasten an outer cleat directly below each end rail (A), using glue and 3" deck screws driven through the cleat and into the base and end rail. Fasten the third cleat so it is centered between the outer cleats, flush with the ends of the frame. For this cleat, use glue and 1¼" deck screws driven through the inside surface of the bottom panel and into the top edge of the cleat. After the bottom panel and cleats are installed, cut and install the post cleats (D). These parts have beveled edges so they can fit into each corner of the sandbox, creating pockets that will hold the roof posts. To cut the post cleats, set your circular saw to make a 45° cut, then trim the end of a cedar 2 × 8 so the bevel points in. Now, measure 7" from the top of the

bevel, and mark a cutting line. With your saw still set at 45°, cut at this line, so the bevel slants in toward the first bevel. Flip the 2 × 8 over, and continue cutting cleats, using the same technique. When all four cleats are cut, fasten them in each corner with glue and 1¼" deck screws, driven roughly perpendicular to the boards in the sandbox frame **(photo A).**

CUT & ATTACH THE TOP OF THE SANDBOX FRAME. The top part of the sandbox frame is made up of the corner boards and the ledges that create the seating area around the perimeter of the sandbox. Cutting these parts involves cutting some miters. The easiest, most accurate way to cut the top parts for the frame is by laying boards directly in place and using the other parts of the framework to trace cutting lines. Start by cutting the corner braces (F): cut two pieces of cedar 2 × 8 to 7¼" in length, then draw a diagonal cutting line on each board. Cut along the cutting line of each board to create four 7¼" triangular pieces.

Make decorative cutouts on the roof aprons with a jig saw.

you made the post cleats for the base. Fasten the top post cleats with glue and screws. To make the top panel (L), use the other half of the cedar plywood panel that was cut for the base. Fasten it to the top frame with glue and 1¼" deck screws. Cut the end aprons (N) and side aprons (O) to length from 1 × 6 cedar. Cut 4¾"-radius semi-circles, spaced at 5" intervals, into the aprons to dress up the design. Cut the semi-circles with a jig saw **(photo C)**. Attach the aprons to the end and side frames, so the tops are flush with the top panel, with glue and 1¼" screws.

APPLY FINISHING TOUCHES. Cut the posts (P) to length from 2 × 2 cedar. Test the fit of the posts: set a post in each corner-brace cutout; then, set the roof onto the tops of the posts **(photo D)**. Sand all surfaces of the sandbox and cover smooth, then apply several coats of clear wood sealer. Move the sandbox to its planned location, then fill with sand.

Each corner brace has a 1½" square cutout for a 2 × 2 roof post. To mark positions for these cutouts, use a 2 × 4 scrap to mark reference lines 1½" inside each of the short arms of the triangle. Then, set a cedar 2 × 2 on end at the corners where each set of reference lines joins. Trace around the 2 × 2 to make a cutout on each end brace. Drill a starter hole at each corner of the cutout, then cut all four cutouts with a jig saw. Fasten the corner braces in each corner of the frame using glue and 3" deck screws, countersunk slightly. Now, lay a piece of 2 × 6 cedar next to one of the corner braces, so it is resting flat on the frame and the edge is flush with the inside edge of the corner brace. From below, trace the outside edges of the end and side rails onto the underside of the 2 × 6 to mark cutting lines for a corner seat (G). Cut along the cutting lines with a circular saw, then mark and cut the three other corner seats. Install them so the edges are butted up against the corner

braces, using glue and 3" screws. Finally, cut the ledges (H) slightly longer than the finished length (see *Cutting List*, page 59) from 2 × 4 cedar. Lay each ledge in place, so it spans between two corners, with the outside edge flush with the outside of the sandbox. Mark cutting lines where ledges intersect the corner seats **(photo B)**; cut the ledges with a circular saw, then install with glue and screws. Also drive two 8d galvanized finish nails through each joint for extra strength.

BUILD THE ROOF. The roof is made in much the same way as the sandbox frame. Cut the end frames (I) and side frames (J), then position the end frames between the side frames, and fasten with 3" deck screws and glue at each joint (drill countersunk pilot holes before driving screws). Cut the stringer (M) from 2 × 2 cedar and fasten it between the frame ends, halfway between sides, with glue and screws. Cut the top post cleats (K) to length from 1 × 2 cedar, cutting 45° bevels on both ends, the same way

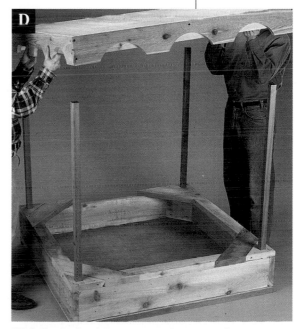

With the ends of the posts in the corner brace cutouts, slip the roof over the top post ends.

Kids' Game Table

A cutout game board and concealed storage box make this child-size game table a great way to keep your parent-size tables clear.

CONSTRUCTION MATERIALS

Quantity	Lumber
1	¾" × 4 × 8' plywood

The perfect table for any board game, this table features ample storage, in addition to sturdy construction and specialized design. The top contains a cutout game table that easily pulls out to reveal a storage space below. This concealed storage area is perfect for holding the small game pieces that always seem to end up on the floor or under the couch. We designed the game table at a convenient height for most children. The kids will appreciate this game table because it is fun. You will appreciate it because it gives the children a specific area just for games, keeping the coffee table and the living room floor free from clutter.

OVERALL SIZE:
20" HIGH
36" WIDE
35" LONG

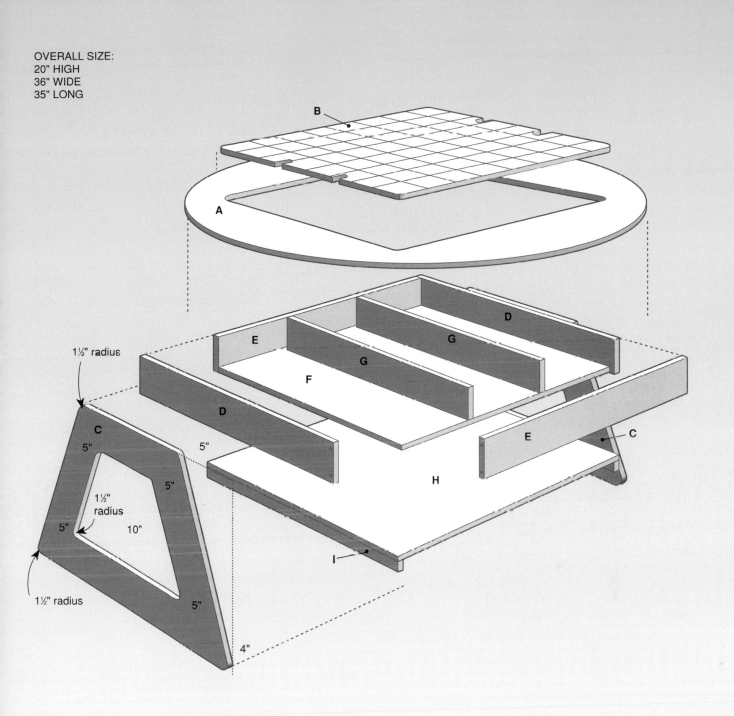

1½" radius

1½"
radius

1½" radius

B

A

E

D

G

G

F

C

D

E

C

H

I

C

5"

5"

5"

5"

10"

5"

4"

Cutting List

Key	Part	Dimension	Pcs.	Material
A	Top	¾ × 36 × 36"	1	Plywood
B	Game board	¾ × 22¼ × 22¼"	1	Plywood
C	Leg	¾ × 18 × 24"	2	Plywood
D	Side	¾ × 4 × 24"	2	Plywood
E	End	¾ × 4 × 22½"	2	Plywood

Cutting List

Key	Part	Dimension	Pcs.	Material
F	Bottom	¾ × 22½ × 22½"	1	Plywood
G	Divider	¾ × 3¼ × 22½"	2	Plywood
H	Fixed shelf	¾ × 22½ × 24"	1	Plywood
I	Cleat	¾ × 1½ × 20"	2	Plywood

Materials: Glue, wood screws (#6 × 1¼", #6 × 2"), finishing materials.

Note: Measurements reflect the actual size of dimensional lumber.

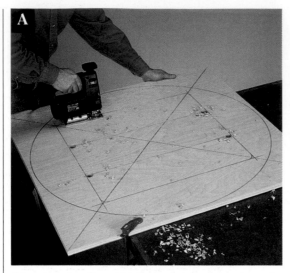

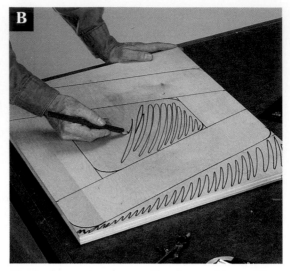

After drawing the guidelines, cut the game board cutout from the top with a jig saw.

Shade the waste areas on the plywood to avoid confusion when cutting the leg to shape.

Directions: Game Table

BUILD THE TOP. The top starts as a large square. You must lay out cutting guidelines carefully to achieve the finished circular shape and built-in game board. Begin by cutting the top (A) to size from ¾"-thick plywood. Mark the centers of each edge on the 36 × 36" square top, and use a straightedge to draw lines connecting the centers on opposing edges. The point where the lines intersect is the center of the board. Draw marks along each edge, 11⅛" to each side of the edge centers. Use a straightedge to draw lines connecting these marks on opposing edges, creating a square with 22¼" sides on the top. This square is the outline of the game board (B). To cut the top to its finished circular shape, you need to build a makeshift compass. Drive a wire nail into the table centerpoint. Tie one end

of a piece of string around the nail and the other around a pencil—the string should measure 17½" in length when tied to the nail and pencil. Pull the pencil outward until the string is taut, and mark the line on the material as you circle the nail. The result is a circle with a 17½" radius. Use a compass to draw a curve with a ¾" radius in each corner of the game board cutting lines. To make finger grips for the game board, mark two points along two opposing sides of the square, 7" in from the corners. Drill 1"-dia. holes at each of the points, then cut along the drawn square with a jig saw to make the game board **(photo A).** Cut around the circle lines to finish the top shape. Lightly sand all

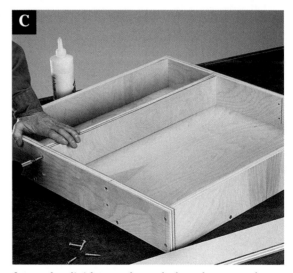

Insert the dividers and attach them between the ends with glue and wood screws.

the edges. Do not sand the edges of the cutout extensively—too much sanding will create large gaps between the game board and the top.

MAKE THE BASE. The information on cutting the legs (C) to shape can be found in the *Diagram*, page 63. When you have one leg cut to shape, just trace around it to create the second leg. Lay out the guidelines for cutting one leg to shape (see *Diagram*, page 63). Use a compass to draw 1½"-radius curves on all the corners.

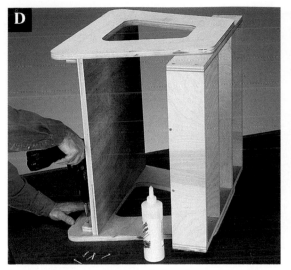

Drive wood screws through the cleats and into the legs to fasten them beneath the fixed shelf.

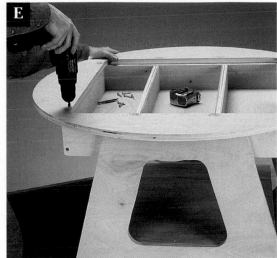

Fasten the top to the storage box with glue and countersunk wood screws.

To avoid confusion when cutting, shade the waste areas **(photo B).** Cut the leg to shape with a jig saw. Draw the cutting guidelines for the second leg, using the finished leg as a tracing template.

MAKE THE STORAGE BOX. The storage box is a simple frame with a plywood bottom that fits directly under the top. Start by cutting the sides (D), ends (E) and bottom (F) to size. Fasten the ends between the sides with glue and countersunk #6 × 2" wood screws, driven through the sides and into the ends. Make sure the outside faces of the ends are flush with the side edges. Position the bottom inside the frame formed by the ends and sides, and fasten it with glue and screws, flush with the bottom of the frame. Cut the dividers (G) to size. To attach the dividers, mark lines on the ends, 6½" from the sides. Drill evenly spaced pilot holes for #6 × 2" wood screws on this line. Fasten the dividers between the ends with glue and screws **(photo C).**

ATTACH THE LEGS. Draw lines on the top, side edges of the storage box, 5" from each end. Align one leg between these lines so the top edges are flush. Apply glue to the parts, and fasten the leg to the storage box with #6 × 1¼" wood screws, driven through the box side and into the leg. Repeat this procedure with the other leg. Cut the fixed shelf (H) and cleats (I) to size. Use glue and countersunk wood screws to attach the fixed shelf between the legs. The top of the fixed shelf should be 4" from the bottom of the leg. Position a cleat directly under each side of the fixed shelf. With the cleats butting against the bottom of the fixed shelf, fasten them to the inside of the legs with glue and countersunk screws **(photo D).**

APPLY FINISHING TOUCHES. Center the top on the storage box, and drive countersunk #6 × 2" wood screws through the top and down into the top edges of the storage box **(photo E).** Fill all the countersunk screw holes with wood putty, and finish-sand all the surfaces with fine-grit sandpaper. Place the game board in the top cutout. Make sure it is well supported and easy to lift out. Trim the edges and deepen the finger holes by sanding with a drum sander, if necessary. Remove the game board. Prime the surfaces, then paint the game table (we used a semigloss latex enamel paint). Although you can leave the game table blank, we sponge-painted it with rows of 1½"-wide squares for playing checkers or chess **(photo F).**

Sponge-paint a checkerboard onto the game board for built-in fun.

Kids' Bathroom Stool

Perfectly sized for children as they put on their shoes or stand at the sink to brush their teeth, this stool makes it easy to be small.

Well suited for a bathroom or a bedroom, this versatile stool can give your child just the lift he or she needs. Made from solid red oak, it features a

sturdy four-legged construction that won't wobble or tip. It is low enough to the ground that a typical toddler can use it as a dressing seat when struggling to put on shoes and socks. It is just high enough to give the added boost he or she needs to reach the sink. Because it is lightweight and portable, it can even move around the house with your child to help with a wide array of activities and chores.

The warm tones of the solid oak and the simple lines of the design make this bathroom

stool an attractive accent in any room. But part of its beauty comes from the ease with which it can be built. The pedestal-style base is made with four basic 1 × 6 legs butted against a central post that is made from four 1 × 2s. The round seat is simply made from two semicircular pieces of oak 1 × 6, butted together along their straight edges. Even the cleats that fit under the seat are easy to cut with a power miter box or a miter box and backsaw.

CONSTRUCTION MATERIALS	
Quantity	**Lumber**
1	1 × 2" × 4' red oak
1	1 × 6" × 6' red oak

66

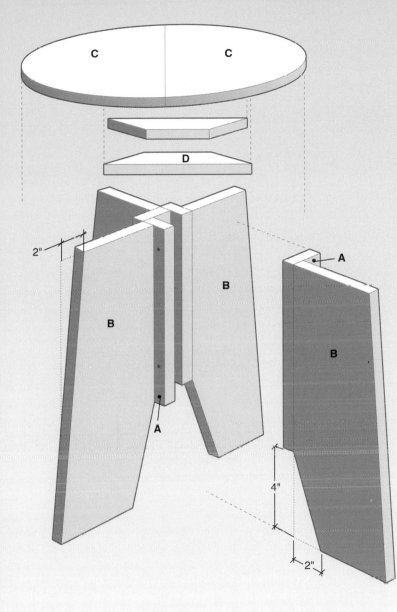

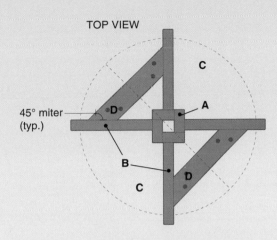

TOP VIEW

45° miter
(typ.)

C

D

A

B

C

D

SIDE VIEW

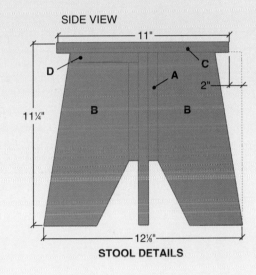

11"

D

C

A

2"

11¼"

B

B

12⅛"

STOOL DETAILS

2"

B

B

B

A

B

A

A

4"

2"

Cutting List				
Key	**Part**	**Dimension**	**Pcs.**	**Material**
A	Post side	¾ × 1½ × 6½"	4	Red oak
B	Leg	¾ × 5½ × 10½"	4	Red oak
C	Seat section	¾ × 5½ × 11"	2	Red oak
D	Cleat	¾ × 1½ × 6"	2	Red oak

Materials: Glue, brass wood screws (#6 × 1¼", #6 × 2"), ⅜"-dia. oak wood plugs, finishing materials.

Specialty Items: Power miter box (optional), compass.

Note: Measurements reflect the actual size of dimensional lumber.

Directions:
Bathroom Stool

MAKE THE LEGS. The four legs for the stools are cut from 1 × 6 oak. The legs are attached to a central post made from four pieces of oak 1 × 2. Cut the legs (B) to size. Each leg is trimmed on the sides, removing two triangular strips to create a tapered appearance. Draw cutting lines onto each leg **(photo A).** To make the lines, mark points 2" in from the inside, bottom corner of each leg, on the bottom edges. Mark a point 4" up from the same corner, on the inside edge of each leg. Connect the points to make cutting lines. To mark the triangular cutouts on the outside edges of the legs, mark points 2" in from the top, outside corners, on the top edge of each leg. Connect each point to the outside, bottom corner of the leg. Cut out the two triangular shapes from each leg, using a jig saw or circular saw.

MAKE THE CENTRAL POST. Cut the four post sides (A) to length. Use a straightedge to draw reference lines ¾" in from one side edge of each post (these lines mark the inside edge of the adjoining post where it butts against each post). Drill two pilot holes for #6 × 2" wood screws between each reference line and the edge of each post— drill the pilot holes 2" down from the top and 2" up from the bottom. Counterbore each pilot hole to accept a ⅜"-dia. oak wood plug—the counterbored faces will be the outside faces of

Draw cutting lines on both edges of each leg to create a tapered appearance. Cut with a jig saw or circular saw.

the post sides. Also drill two plain pilot holes on the back of each post side, ⅜" in from the opposite edge of the counterbored pilot holes (these pilot holes are for the screws you will use to connect each post side to a leg). Drill 1" from the top and bottom edges. Apply glue to the inside edge of one leg, and butt a post side against the leg, so the tops of the pieces are flush. Extend the pilot holes at the inside edge of each post into the leg, then fasten the leg to the post with #6 × 2" brass wood screws—always use brass fasteners when working with oak. Fasten each leg to a post side.

ASSEMBLE THE PEDESTAL. To assemble the stool pedestal, apply glue to the edge of each post side that is flush with a leg. Position a pair of leg/post sides together so the tops are flush and the counterbored pilot holes in the post sides are centered on the glued edge of the adjoining assembly. Drive #6 × 1¼" brass wood screws through

the pilot holes in the posts and into the edge of the adjoining post. Repeat these steps with the rest of the leg assemblies to complete the pedestal **(photo B).**

MAKE THE SEAT SECTIONS. The seat is made from two semicircular boards that are butted together to form a full circle. Cut a piece of 1 × 6 oak into two 11"-long seat sections (C). Lay the seat sections side by side. Use a compass to draw a circle with a 5½" radius on the seat sections. The point of the compass should be positioned between the boards, centered end to end. Cut along the circle with a jig saw to form two semicircles. Attach a belt sander to your worksurface so the belt is perpendicular to the surface, and use it to smooth out the rough spots and contours on the seat sections **(photo C).**

MAKE & ATTACH CLEATS. The seat sections are edge-glued together, with the joint reinforced by a pair of wood cleats

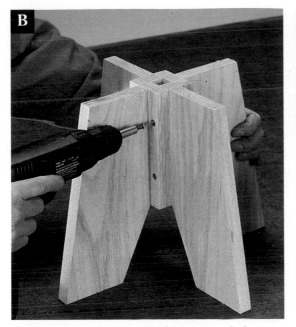

Connect the posts with wood screws and glue to complete the base.

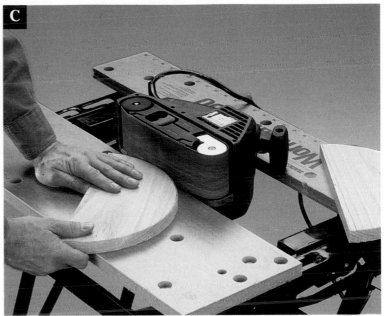

Smooth out the curves on the seat sections with a belt sander after you cut them to shape.

that fit between the legs at the top of the pedestal, and span the seam between the seat sections. Cut the cleats (D) to length from 1 × 2 oak. Trim off the ends of each cleat at a 45° angle with a miter box (see *Diagram,* page 67). Drill a pair of staggered, counterbored pilot holes near each end of each cleat (see *Diagram*) for fastening the cleats to the seat sections. Position the cleats so they fit between pairs of legs, flush with the tops, on opposite sides of the pedestal. Drill counterbored pilot holes and attach the cleats between the legs with #6 × 1¼" brass wood screws— make sure the tops of the cleats are flush with the tops of the legs and central post.

ATTACH THE SEAT. Apply glue to the straight edges of the seat sections, then butt them together to form a circle. Tape the seam with masking tape on the top, then lay the seat top down on a flat worksurface. Invert the pedestal, then set it on

top of the underside of the seat. Make sure the seat overhang is equal on all sides, and the seam of the seat falls across the centers of the cleats. Drive #6 × 1¼" screws through the cleats and into the seat. Drill counterbored pilot holes, and attach the seat to the top edges of the legs with one #6 × 2" screw driven through the seat and into the top of each leg.

APPLY FINISHING TOUCHES. Fill the counterbored screw holes in the seat with glued oak plugs **(photo D),** then sand the plugs level with the wood surface. Finish-sand all surfaces with 180-grit sandpaper. Apply wood stain (we used light oak wipe-on stain). After the stain has dried, apply two or three coats of polyurethane to protect the wood.

Insert glued oak plugs into the counterbored screw holes on the top of the seat.

Bookworm Study Set

*A matching lamp base and bookends
make studying fun for young learners.*

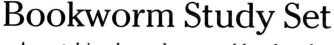

CONSTRUCTION MATERIALS

Quantity	Lumber
1	¼" × 2 × 4' plywood
1	¾" × 2 × 4' plywood
1	1 × 2" × 6' pine

The engaging cartoon bookworm that weaves its way through this lamp base and matching set of bookends will help your kids look forward to study time. Along with sending the positive message that learning is fun, this study set also fulfills a valuable, practical function by bringing additional light and storage to your child's bedroom.

This study set project is a learning experience for the parent or grandparent who builds it, as well. Equal parts craft and carpentry, cutting the intricate bookworm shapes and applying the decorative painted finish will teach you a lot about your own level of enthusiasm for detail-oriented crafts. If you enjoy it, you may have discovered a new hobby that could lead quickly to more intricate scrollsaw or bandsaw projects. But even if you don't particularly enjoy the process, you'll still have a special gift to give to a special child or grandchild.

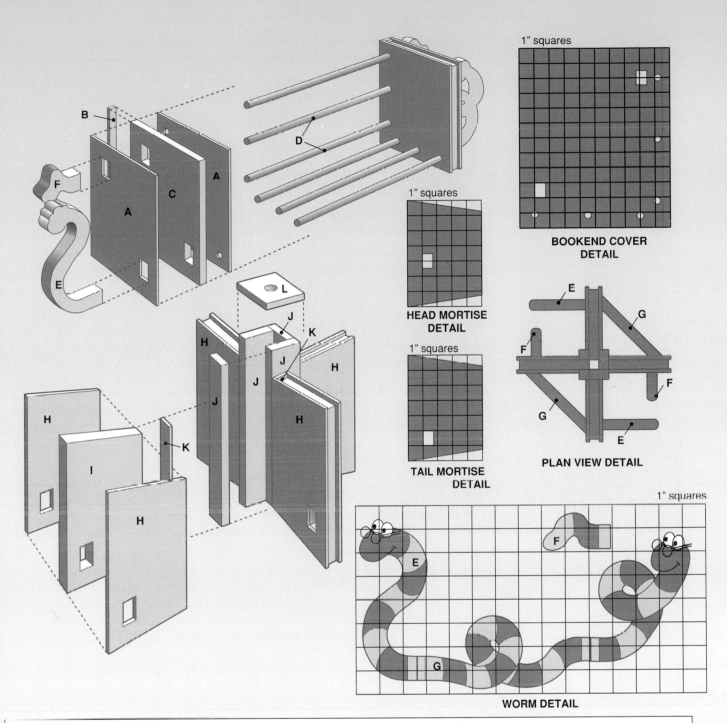

1" squares

BOOKEND COVER DETAIL

1" squares

HEAD MORTISE DETAIL

1" squares

TAIL MORTISE DETAIL

PLAN VIEW DETAIL

1" squares

WORM DETAIL

Bookends Cutting List

Key	Part	Dimension	Pcs.	Material
A	Bookend cover	¼ × 10 × 12"	4	Plywood
B	Spine	¼ × ¾ × 12"	2	Plywood
C	Page	¾ × 9½ × 11¾"	2	Plywood
D	Dowel	½ × 19½"	6	Dowel
E	Worm head	¾ × 5½ × 7"	4	Plywood
F	Worm tail	¾ × 2½ × 3"	4	Plywood

Lamp Base Cutting List

Key	Part	Dimension	Pcs.	Material
G	Worm middle	¾ × 4 × 7½"	2	Plywood
H	Lamp cover	¼ × 5 × 8"	8	Plywood
I	Lamp page	¾ × 4½ × 7¾"	4	Plywood
J	Post	¾ × 1½ × 11¼"	4	Pine
K	Lamp spine	¼ × ¾ × 6½"	4	Plywood
L	Post cap	¾ × 3½ × 3½"	1	Plywood

Materials: Glue, epoxy, #4 × 1¼" wood screws, 1" wire brads, ½"-dia. dowels, lamp hardware kit with a 12"+ tube, finishing materials.

Specialty items: Flat wood file, fine scrolling jig saw blade, coping saw.

Note: Measurements reflect the actual size of dimensional lumber.

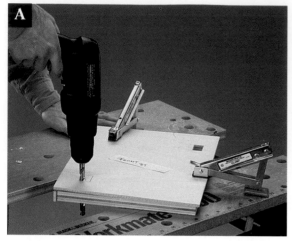

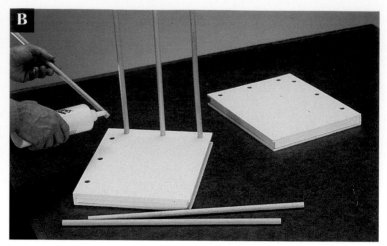

Drill a starter hole, then cut the mortises for the bookworm with a jig saw.

Prime or prime and paint the bookends, then glue dowels into the dowel holes to connect the bookends.

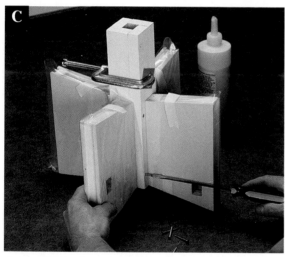

Assemble the lamp base by attaching the posts.

Directions:
Bookworm Study Set

BUILD THE BOOKENDS. The bookends are made by building three-part "book" assemblies from plywood and connecting them with dowels. Cut the bookend covers (A), spines (B) and pages (C) to size. Sand all parts smooth. Use glue and 1" wire brads to attach the spines to one edge of each page. Center the spines on the pages so ⅛" of the spine extends beyond the top and bottom of each page. When the spines are attached, designate the inside and outside covers,

and mark them accordingly. Each outside cover contains two ¾"-wide × 1"-high mortises to hold the ends of the bookworm parts. Mark the mortise locations (see *Diagram*, page 71) on the outside covers, then clamp each outside cover to a page and spine. Make sure the covers extend past the pages ¼" on the front and ⅛" on the top and bottom edge. Place the clamped assembly, page down, on a worksurface, and drill starter holes for the mortises, through both the outside covers and the pages **(photo A).** Cut the mortises into both parts with a jig saw. With the covers and pages still clamped together, use a flat wood file to file the edges of the mortises so they are square. Clamp the inside covers together, and mark centers for the dowels (see *Diagram*, page 71). Note that the dowels on the bottom edge form a line that slopes downward slightly, and the dowels on the back edge of the bookends tilt back slightly from bottom to top (this helps prevent books from falling out of the bookends). Drill a ½"-dia. hole at each centerpoint. Now, unclamp the inside covers,

and position each inside cover over a page, maintaining the same ⅛" and ¼" setbacks established when cutting the mortises. Be careful not to confuse the front and back of the inside covers, then clamp each cover to a page and extend the ½"-dia. holes all the way through the page. Unclamp the parts and wipe the surfaces clean. Now, assemble the two books by sandwiching a page between each pair of covers, making sure the mortises and dowel holes are aligned. Bond the books together with glue and 1" wire brads. Set the heads of the brads and fill the holes and the exposed plywood edges with wood putty. Sand all surfaces, then apply a heavy layer of white primer to each book. Cut the dowels (D) to size, apply glue to the ends, and insert them into the dowel holes **(photo B)**. After the glue dries, mask the exposed page edges with masking tape, then paint the covers with enamel paint (we decided to leave the dowels with a natural color, so we also masked the ends of the dowels where they meet the covers before painting).

Trace the bookworm pattern onto plywood, then cut along the cutting line with a jig saw fitted with a fine scrolling blade.

MAKE THE LAMP BASE. The lamp is also designed with the book-and-bookworm motif. The base uses four smaller books that are foreshortened from front to back. The spine of each book is attached to a 1 × 2 post, then the post sections are joined together to form a hollow post that allows room for the lamp kit. Cut the lamp covers (H), lamp pages (I) and lamp spines (K) to size. Trim the tops and bottoms of the lamp covers and pages so they slope toward the center of the book ¾" from the front to the back (see *Diagram*). Attach the lamp spines to the lamp pages with glue and 1" wire brads. Assemble pairs of covers with pages the same way as with the bookend covers. Cut a mortise all the way through each "book" according to the positioning shown in the *Diagram*: cut two books with head mortises, and two with tail mortises. Make sure the covers with the head mortises are opposite one another when the base is assembled. Cut the posts (J) and post cap (L) to size. Attach a post to the spine of each book, with glue and #4 × 1¼" screws driven through

the posts and into the spines. The bottoms of the spines and posts should be flush, and the inside edge of each post should be ½" from the left side of the book (when the book is standing upright). Finish-sand each book assembly, and apply primer and paint—we suggest you use the same color schemes used for the bookends. After the paint dries, tape plastic over the nonmating surfaces of the assemblies for scratch protection. Apply glue to the posts, and secure them together into a hollow lamp post **(photo C)** with #4 × 1¼" screws (see *Diagram*). Remove plastic protection. Drill a ⅜"-dia. hole through the center of the post cap for a threaded lamp tube (check the diameter of the tube in your lamp kit, and make sure this hole matches it). Center the cap over the posts and fasten it with glue and wire brads.

MAKE THE BOOKWORMS. The easiest way to draw the serpentine shapes for the bookworms is to transfer the grid pattern from the *Diagram* onto a piece of graph paper to full size, then cut out the shape in the paper

to form a template. Lay the template over a piece of ¾" plywood, and trace around it. Mark cutting lines (the worm will be divided into sections) and draw guidelines for painting, then cut out the shape with a jig saw and fine scrolling blade **(photo D).** Drill holes in the internal cutouts, and cut them to shape with a coping saw. Cut worm sections for both the bookends and the lamp base (For the lamp base, miter-cut the worm middle ends at 45° angles). Sand the edges smooth, fill with putty, finish-sand, then paint the bookworm (we followed the cartoon pattern, using craft paint in the colors shown).

APPLY FINISHING TOUCHES. Glue the bookworm heads and tails into the mortises in the bookends and lamp base, following the *Diagram*. Tack the bookworm middle sections in the lamp base in place with quick-setting epoxy, then secure each end of the middle sections with a 1" wire brad driven through a pilot hole **(photo E).** Install the lamp hardware kit according to the manufacturer's directions.

Drive wire brads through the worm middle and into the lamp covers.

Deck Chair

Lean back and soak in the sun on this supremely comfortable cedar chair for your deck or for the beach.

CONSTRUCTION MATERIALS

Quantity	Lumber
2	1 × 2" × 8' cedar
5	1 × 4" × 8' cedar
1	1 × 6" × 6' cedar
1	2 × 2" × 6' cedar

Angled perfectly for sun-bathing on a deck, in the yard or at the beach, this sturdy, comfortable beach chair is one of the cleverest and most convenient pieces of outdoor furniture you can find. This deck chair is made of two parts that disassemble easily and quickly for storage or transport. The long back section is a simple frame made with sides, slats and stretchers. The seat section fits between the back slats to create a stable, versatile chair. When the sun goes down, just pull the seat section out, slip it into the back section, and carry it away. When you lean back and enjoy the sun, you will be amazed at how comfortable this chair really is, and how easy it was to build.

74

OVERALL SIZE:
35" HIGH
24" WIDE
40" LONG

5" radius

1" squares

PART D DETAIL

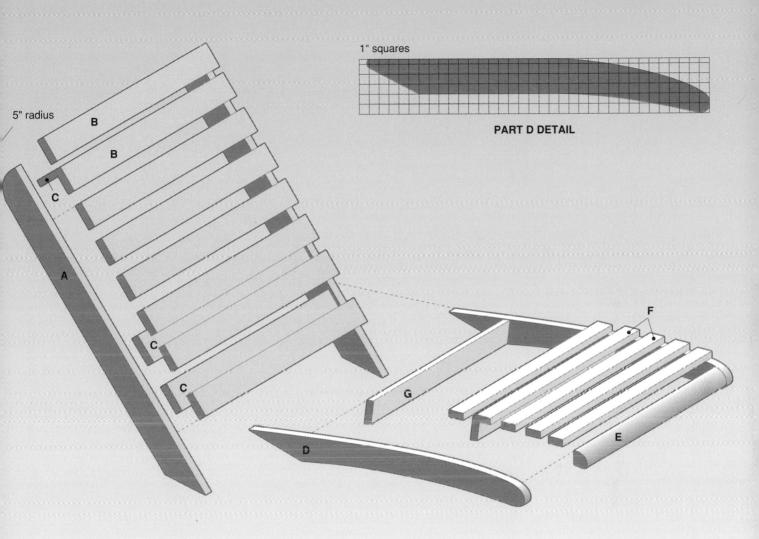

Cutting List				
Key	**Part**	**Dimension**	**Pcs.**	**Material**
A	Side	¾ × 3½ × 49"	2	Cedar
B	Back slat	¾ × 3½ × 24"	8	Cedar
C	Stretcher	¾ × 3½ × 22¼"	3	Cedar
D	Leg	¾ × 5½ × 35"	2	Cedar

Cutting List				
Key	**Part**	**Dimension**	**Pcs.**	**Material**
E	Front spreader	1½ × 1½ × 20½"	1	Cedar
F	Seat slat	¾ × 1½ × 22¼"	5	Cedar
G	Stringer	¾ × 3½ × 20½"	2	Cedar

Materials: Moisture-resistant glue, deck screws (1⅝", 2"), finishing materials.

Note: Measurements reflect the actual thickness of dimensional lumber.

75

Directions: Deck Chair

MAKE THE SIDES. The sides are long boards that serve as the main structural members on both sides of the back frame. Each side is cut to shape with one slanted end and one curved end. Start by cutting the sides (A) to the length shown in the *Cutting List*. Clamp the sides together, edge to edge, so their ends are flush. To cut the sides to shape, first draw reference lines for the bottoms of the sides: at one end of each side, use a combination square to draw a straight line at a 45°

A

A makeshift wood strip compass can be used to mark rounded cutting lines.

angle from the inside edge corner toward the opposite corner, 3½" in from the ends. On the other end of each side, use a compass to draw a 5"-radius curve that forms the top (see *Diagram*). For large-radius curves, use a thin, straight piece of scrap wood as a homemade compass. First, mark the centers of each side, 5" down from the tops of the sides and 1¾" in from the edges. Drive a nail through the scrap piece on one center-point. Slide a pencil through a hole in the scrap piece, 5" from the nail. The curves should start at the top, inside corners of the sides and end on the outside edge, 4½" down from the top edge **(photo A).** While the sides are still square, mark reference lines to help you position the two bottom slats and two bottom stretchers. Mark reference lines on the side faces, 7½", 8½", 14¾" and 15¾" up from the bottoms of the sides. These reference lines will be used later in the assembly process. Cut the sides to shape with a jig saw.

ATTACH THE BACK SLATS. Slats are attached on the front edges of the sides to form the back

frame. Make sure you carefully align the bottom two slats with their reference lines before attaching them—the gap must be wide enough to accommodate the seat section. Begin by cutting the back slats (B) to size. Draw reference lines at each end of the slats, ⁷⁄₁₆" in from the ends. Drill two evenly spaced pilot holes through each reference line. Position the sides on their edges so the flat edges are facing up. Use glue and 2" deck screws to fasten one back slat at the top (curved) ends of the sides, making sure the edges are flush. Position two slats so they align with the reference lines 7½" and 14¾" up from the bottom (slanted) ends of the sides. The bottom edges of the slats should be flush with the lines. Attach the slats with moisture-resistant glue and 2" deck screws, making sure to maintain a 3¾"-wide gap between slats **(photo B).** Then, starting at the tops of the sides, attach the remaining slats with glue and deck screws, using a scrap 1 × 2 as a spacer to maintain the gap between slats.

ATTACH THE STRETCHERS. The stretchers are attached between the sides to add struc-

B

Position two slats so their bottom edges align with the reference lines, then attach them to the sides.

C

Fit the stretchers between the sides so they are flush with the rear edges, and fasten them with glue and screws.

Soften the sharp corners of the slats with a router and roundover bit or a sander.

Round over the front spreader to follow the profiles of the legs.

tural support and brace the seat section when it is fitted in place. Cut the stretchers (C) to size. Position the back frame on your worksurface so the slats are on the bottom. Fit one stretcher between the sides, 4½" in from the top (curved) ends, and fasten it with moisture-resistant glue and 2" deck screws. Make sure this top stretcher is attached so its long edges are flush with the edges of the sides. The remaining two stretchers are attached so their faces are flush with the back edge of the sides. Position these stretchers on the reference lines, 8½" and 15¾" in from the bottoms of the sides, and attach them with glue and 2" deck screws **(photo C).** It is crucial that these bottom stretchers be separated by a 3¾"-wide gap; otherwise, the seat section might not fit securely into the back frame. Round over the top faces of all the slats with a router and a ⅜"-dia. roundover bit **(photo D).**

MAKE THE SEAT SECTION. Cut the legs (D) to length. Draw a grid with 1" squares, and transfer the grid pattern from the *Di-*

agram on page 75 to the workpiece. Cut the leg to shape with a jig saw, and sand the edges. Trace the finished leg onto the uncut leg, and cut it to shape. The slanted end of each leg is the rear end, and sits flush against the floor when the chair is assembled. The front ends of the legs are slightly rounded so your legs will be comfortable. Draw reference lines across one face of each leg, 6" and 20" in from the back (slanted) ends. These reference lines mark the position of the stringers (G). Cut the stringers to size, and fasten them between the legs with moisture-resistant glue and 2" deck screws. The rear faces of the stringers should be flush with the reference lines. Countersink the screws so the screw heads are slightly recessed. Cut the front spreader (E) to size, and fasten it between the legs so the front edge is flush with the fronts of the legs. Use a belt sander to round the front spreader to match the curved profile of the fronts of the legs **(photo E).** Cut the seat slats (F) to size. Drill pilot holes at each

end of the slats for 2" deck screws. Starting 1½" in from the back of the spreader, attach the slats with moisture-resistant glue and deck screws, maintaining even spacing by using an unattached slat as a 1½"-wide spacer **(photo F).**

APPLY FINISHING TOUCHES. Finish-sand all the surfaces of the beach chair, taking care to smooth out any rough or sharp edges. Wipe the wood clean, then apply an exterior-rated finish to the project to preserve the wood. We used a redwood-tinted, exterior penetrating wood stain.

Use a scrap as a spacer for setting gaps as you attach the seat slats.

Fireplace Box

This rustic firewood storage box nestles into your fireplace hearth, keeping all your kindling and cordwood in one neat package.

CONSTRUCTION MATERIALS

Quantity	Lumber
1	1 × 3" × 6' cedar
2	1 × 4" × 8' cedar
8	1" × 6 × 8' cedar

A simple storage box made from cedar, this fireplace box allows you to store your wood where it is needed—near the fireplace. It's an attractive project that looks great in any vacation home. The main compartment holds cordwood and kindling, and a handy shelf at the top is used to store tinder and matches.

We modeled this fireplace box after Early American styles, which served homes so reliably all those years ago. There was very little to improve upon; this project is easy to build and easy to look at. And if you have small children, you can even equip it with a hasp and lock to keep matches out of reach.

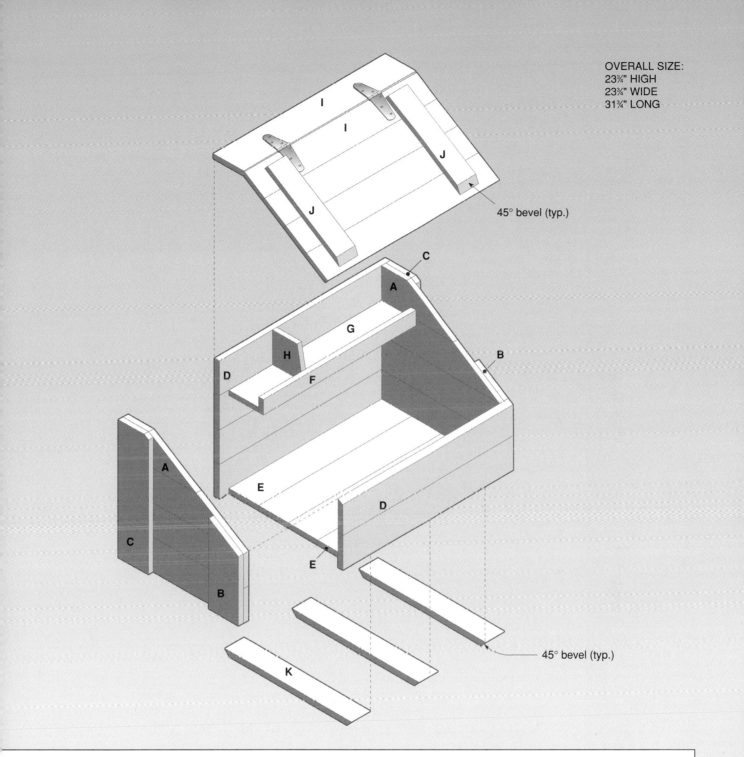

OVERALL SIZE:
23¾" HIGH
23¾" WIDE
31¾" LONG

45° bevel (typ.)

45° bevel (typ.)

A B C D E F G H I J K

Cutting List				
Key	Part	Dimension	Pcs.	Material
A	Side board	⅞ × 5½ × 22"	8	Cedar
B	Front post	⅞ × 5½ × 15"	2	Cedar
C	Rear post	⅞ × 5½ × 22"	2	Cedar
D	Front/back	⅞ × 5½ × 31¾"	6	Cedar
E	Floor slat	⅞ × 5½ × 28¼"	4	Cedar
F	Shelf front	⅞ × 2½ × 28¼"	1	Cedar

Cutting List				
Key	Part	Dimension	Pcs.	Material
G	Shelf bottom	⅞ × 5½ × 28¼"	1	Cedar
H	Divider	⅞ × 5½ × 5½"	1	Cedar
I	Top board	⅞ × 5½ × 32"	5	Cedar
J	Support	⅞ × 3½ × 20"	2	Cedar
K	Skid	⅞ × 3½ × 23½"	3	Cedar

Materials: Deck screws (1⅝", 2"), 4" strap hinges (2), finishing materials.

Note: Measurements reflect the actual thickness of dimensional lumber.

79

Use a circular saw to make angled trim cuts in the box sides.

Use a belt sander to extend the slant of the sides onto the top edge of the front board.

Directions:
Fireplace Box

MAKE THE SIDES. Each side of the kindling box is made by attaching four side boards edge to edge to form 22 × 22" square panels. After the sides are joined to posts at the top and bottom, each side is cut with a circular saw to produce the slanted profile of the box sides. Start by cutting the side boards (A), front posts (B) and rear posts (C) to size. Sand all parts after cutting to smooth out any rough spots. Clamp the side boards together in two groups of four, making sure the edges are flush. Position a front post and rear post at the ends of each group of side boards. The rear posts should be flush with

the side boards at all edges, and the front posts should be flush with the front and bottom edges of the sides. Drive 1⅝" deck screws through the side boards and into the front posts and rear posts. Countersink the screws slightly to recess the screw heads, and unclamp the workpieces. To cut the sides to shape, draw a cutting line from the front edge to the back of each side. Mark the cutting lines, starting on the tops of the sides, 4⅝" in from the back edges, and running down to the top of the second lowest board at the front edge. Use a circular saw to cut along the cutting lines **(photo A).** If any screws have been placed along the cutting line, remove them prior to cutting the sides.

ATTACH THE FRONT & BACK BOARDS. The front and back boards close in the box frame. Start by cutting the front/back boards (D) to size. Position two boards at the front of the sides, and four in the back. Attach the boards to the sides with 2" deck screws, driven through

the front/back boards and into the sides. Use a belt sander to extend the slanted profiles of the sides onto the top board at the front of the box **(photo B).**

INSTALL THE FLOOR SLATS. Cut the floor slats (E) to size, and fit them into the bin. Make sure the bin is square by checking the corners with a framing square. Adjust as needed. Fasten the floor slats to the bin by driving 2" deck screws through the bottom edges of the box and into the floor slats.

MAKE THE SHELF. The shelf fits in the top section of the bin and is used for storing matches and tinder. Start by cutting the shelf front (F), shelf bottom (G) and divider (H) to size. The divider has a slightly slanted front edge. To cut the divider to shape, mark a point on one edge, ⅜" in from one corner. Mark another point on an adjacent edge, 4⅜" away from the same corner. Draw a cutting line connecting the two points, and cut with a jig saw. Next, butt the shelf front against one long edge of the bottom. Make sure the ends are flush, and

TIP

Always make sure that firewood is dry and insect-free before storing it inside your home. One good way to help ensure that there are no big surprises hiding inside the wood you bring into your house is to store only split wood firewood in your storage box: generally, if wood is badly infested you will be able to see it when it is split into quarters or halves.

drive 2" deck screws through the face of the shelf front and into the edge of the shelf bottom. Position the divider on the shelf bottom, 8" in from one end. Make sure the slanted front edge of the divider faces the shelf front. Drive deck screws through the shelf bottom and shelf front, and into the divider. Place the shelf assembly in the bin. The top edge of the divider should be flush with the top edges of the box. Attach the shelf by driving 2" deck screws through the back and sides of the bin, and into the shelf edges **(photo C).**

MAKE THE LID. Cut the top boards (I) and supports (J) to size. Fasten one top board to the top of the bin so the back edges are flush and the top board overhangs the ends by ⅛". Drive 2" deck screws through the top board and into the tops of the box and divider. Next, use a circular saw or a power miter saw set at a 45° angle to bevel the front edges of the supports. Clamp the remaining top boards together, edge to edge, so the ends are flush. Center the supports on the top boards. With the beveled ends facing toward the front, drive 1⅝" deck screws through the top boards and into each support, forming the finished lid.

APPLY FINISHING TOUCHES. Cut the skids (K) to size. The skids fit below the bin to raise the box up, allowing air flow below it. Bevel both ends of each skid at 45° with a circular saw or power miter saw. Turn the bin upside down, and use wood screws to attach a skid on each side of the bin bottom, flush with the side edges. Attach the third skid at the center

Attach the shelf at the back of the box so the divider is parallel to the box sides.

Attach the lid to the top of the box with 4" strap hinges.

of the bin bottom. Use a pad sander to remove any splinters from the box. We applied a penetrating stain right after sanding, but you can let the cedar age naturally. Attach 4" strap hinges to the top of the

lid, just inside the supports. Center the lid against the top of the bin, and attach the free ends of the hinges to the fixed top board **(photo D).**

81

Cabin Chair

*Destined to be a family favorite,
this cabin chair combines rustic charm with roomy comfort.*

CONSTRUCTION MATERIALS

Quantity	Lumber
1	1 × 4" × 8' pine
3	1 × 6" × 8' pine
3	2 × 4" × 8' pine
1	2 × 6" × 10' pine

A comfortable armchair on a pleasant summer evening is one of life's great pleasures. This roomy, rustic chair is perfect for a porch, deck or even indoors at a hunting lodge or cabin.

The basic design makes this cabin chair a true classic. Four simple pine frames, the back, legs and seat, are joined together with glue and deck screws to create a rugged, good-looking furniture piece. Although the contoured seat is quite comfortable, you can throw some pillows or blankets on the project for added padding. Decorative pine-tree cutouts on the leg frames and back frame add to the down-home charm.

OVERALL SIZE:
36" HIGH
29½" DEEP
36½" WIDE

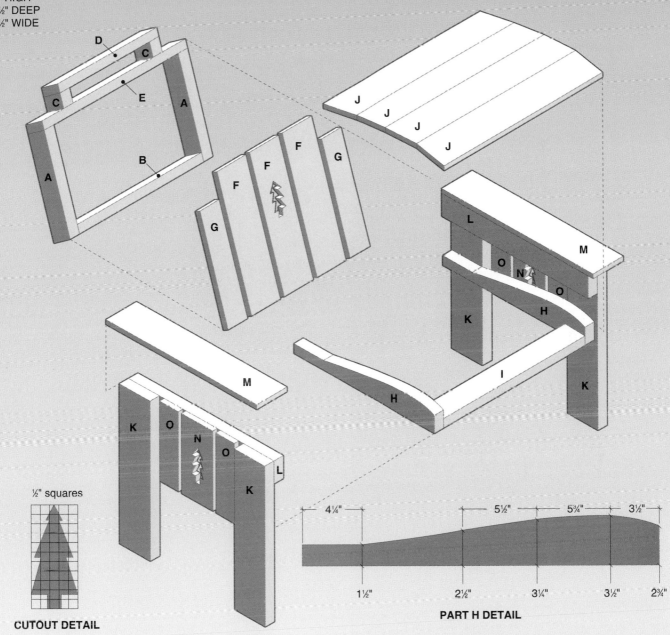

½" squares

CUTOUT DETAIL

PART H DETAIL

Cutting List

Key	Part	Dimension	Pcs.	Material
A	Stile	1½ × 3½ × 17½"	2	Pine
B	Inner rail	1½ × 3½ × 22½"	1	Pine
C	Top block	1½ × 3½ × 2½"	2	Pine
D	Top rail	1½ × 3½ × 17½"	1	Pine
E	Middle rail	1½ × 3½ × 25½"	1	Pine
F	Center slat	¾ × 5½ × 23"	3	Pine
G	End slat	¾ × 3½ × 19"	2	Pine
H	Seat rail	1½ × 3½ × 25½"	2	Pine

Cutting List

Key	Part	Dimension	Pcs.	Material
I	Seat support	1½ × 3½ × 25½"	1	Pine
J	Seat slat	¾ × 5½ × 28½"	4	Pine
K	Leg	1½ × 5½ × 25"	4	Pine
L	Log rail	1½ × 3½ × 27"	2	Pine
M	Armrest	¾ × 5½ × 28"	2	Pine
N	Middle arm slat	¾ × 5½ × 12½"	2	Pine
O	End arm slat	¾ × 3½ × 12½"	4	Pine

Materials: Moisture-resistant wood glue, deck screws (2", 2½"), finishing materials.
Note: Measurements reflect the actual thickness of dimensional lumber.

Directions: Cabin Chair

MAKE THE BACK FRAME. The back frame is made of a large 2 × 4 frame with a smaller 2 × 4 bump-out frame attached to the top for extra support of the backrest slats. Start by cutting the stiles (A) and inner rail (B) to size. After sanding the parts, position the inner rail between the ends of the stiles, and fasten the inner rail with moisture-resistant wood glue and 2½" deck screws driven into coun-terbored pilot holes—counter-bore deeply enough to accept a ⅜"-dia. wood plug. Cut the top blocks (C), top rail (D) and middle rail (E) to size. Use glue and counterbored deck screws to fasten the middle rail to the free ends of the stiles. Fasten the top blocks at the ends of the top rail, using glue and 2½" deck screws driven through the top rail and into the ends of the blocks. Apply glue to the free ends of the top blocks, and po-sition them against the middle rail so their outside edges are 4" in from the ends. Clamp the frames together **(photo A),** and join them by driving 2½" deck screws through the middle rail and into the ends of the top blocks.

MAKE THE SEAT FRAMES. Start by cutting the seat rails (H) to size. Use the *Part H Detail* on page 83 as a reference for marking cutting lines on the seat rails—the tops are curved so the seat slats will slope back for increased comfort. Cut the rails to shape with a jig saw **(photo B),** then clamp the parts together face to face and smooth out the contours with a power sander. Cut the seat sup-port (I) and position it face down between the seat rails, so one long edge is flush with the fronts of the seat rails. Use glue and counterbored 2½" deck screws to fasten the seat sup-port between the seat rails.

MAKE THE LEG FRAMES. Start by cutting the legs (K) and leg rails (L) to size. Set the legs facedown on your worksurface in pairs, 27" apart. Position a leg rail across the tops of each pair of legs so the tops of the legs are flush with the top of the rails and the ends of the rail are flush with the outside edges of the legs. Use glue and 2½" counterbored deck screws, driv-en through the leg rails and into the legs, to attach the parts. Cut the armrests (M) to size, and fasten them on top of the joints between the legs and leg rails so one long edge of each armrest is flush with the inside leg rail and the back edges are flush **(photo C).**

MAKE THE SLATS. Each of the four frames that make up the chair will support slats made from 1× stock. The center slats on the backrest frame and the leg frames fea-ture a pine-tree-shaped cutout. Begin by cutting the center slats (F), end slats (G), seat slats (J), middle arm slats (N) and end arm slats (O) to size. Transfer the pine-tree grid pattern from the *Diagram,* page 83, onto a piece of graph paper, then cut out the

Clamp the top blocks and top rail to the middle rail before attaching the parts with glue and screws.

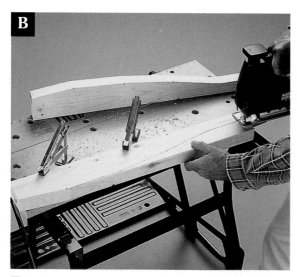

The seat rails are curved on top so the seat will slope for greater comfort. Cut the rails with a jig saw.

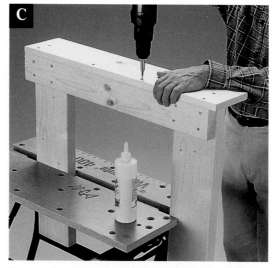

Fasten the armrests to the tops of the leg frames, keeping the back and inside edges flush.

Center the pine-tree templates on the middle arm slats and center slat, and trace the cutout pattern.

Attach the seat frame to the leg frames so the straight bottom edges of the seat rails are perpendicular to the legs.

shape in the paper to form a template. Center the template over one center slat and both middle arm slats, and trace around the cutout shape **(photo D).** Drill a ⅜"-dia. starter hole in the center of each cutout, then cut the pine-tree shapes with a jig saw or coping saw. Sand the edges smooth.

ATTACH THE SEAT & BACK SLATS. It will be easier if you attach the slats to the seat and back frames before assembling the frames—the leg frame slats can't be installed until after all the frames are joined. Use glue and counterbored 2" deck screws to fasten the first seat slat (J) to the seat rails so its front edge extends 1" beyond the front of the frame. Work your way backward, making sure the seat slats butt together edge to edge and are flush with the sides of the seat rails. Drill counterbored pilot holes, and attach the end slats (G) to the back frame with glue and 2" deck screws. The top, bottom and outside edges of the end slats should be flush with the frame. Position the center slats (F) on the back frame, making sure the center slat with the pine-tree cutout is in the middle.

Space the center slats evenly, with a ⅛"-wide gap between slats. Attach the center slats with glue and 2" wood screws. Keep the bottoms of the center slats flush with the bottom of the frame.

ASSEMBLE THE FRAMES. Mark a reference line across the inside faces of the legs, 12½" up from the bottoms. Position the seat frame on one leg frame so the bottom edge of the seat is flush with the reference lines. The front edges of the seat frame and leg frame should be flush, while the back of the seat frame should be 1½" in from the back edge of the leg frame. Apply glue, and clamp the frames together. Attach the frames with 2½" deck screws, driven through the seat rails and into the legs **(photo E).** Repeat this procedure with the other leg frame. Test-fit the back frame between the leg frames. The bottom of the back frame should butt up against the rear seat slat, flush with the bottom edge of the seat. Make sure the ends of the armrests are flush with the rear edges of the back frame, and attach the frames with glue and 2½" deck screws **(photo F).**

ATTACH THE LEG-FRAME SLATS. Position two end arm slats (O) on each leg frame so the bottom ends are flush with the bottoms of the seat rails and the outside edges are 1" in from the legs. Attach the slats to the seat rails and leg rails with glue and 2" deck screws. Position the middle arm slats (N) between the end arm slats, and fasten them to the seat rails and leg rails.

APPLY FINISHING TOUCHES. Glue ⅜"-dia. wood plugs in all counterbores, sand all surfaces, and paint with primer and exterior-rated enamel paint.

Attach the back frame to the leg frames so it butts against the seat frame and slopes back.

Pantry Cabinet

This adjustable cabinet provides the versatility needed to organize your pantry.

PROJECT
POWER TOOLS

M ost pantries are great for storing kitchen supplies or appliances that you don't use every day but still like to have nearby. However, if your pantry itself is poorly organized and inconvenient to use, it winds up as wasted space in your home. To get the most from your pantry, we devised our cabinet for maximum vertical storage capacity. Standing 84" high, the cabinet features three solid shelves for storing heavy goods

and two adjustable shelves to fit large or awkward items. You can use this pantry cabinet as a freestanding unit against a wall or as a divider in a larger pantry. The open construction also means you can identify what you have on hand at a glance. Included in the instructions is a simple option for converting an adjustable shelf into a rack that is perfect for stable storage of wine, soda or other bottled liquids.

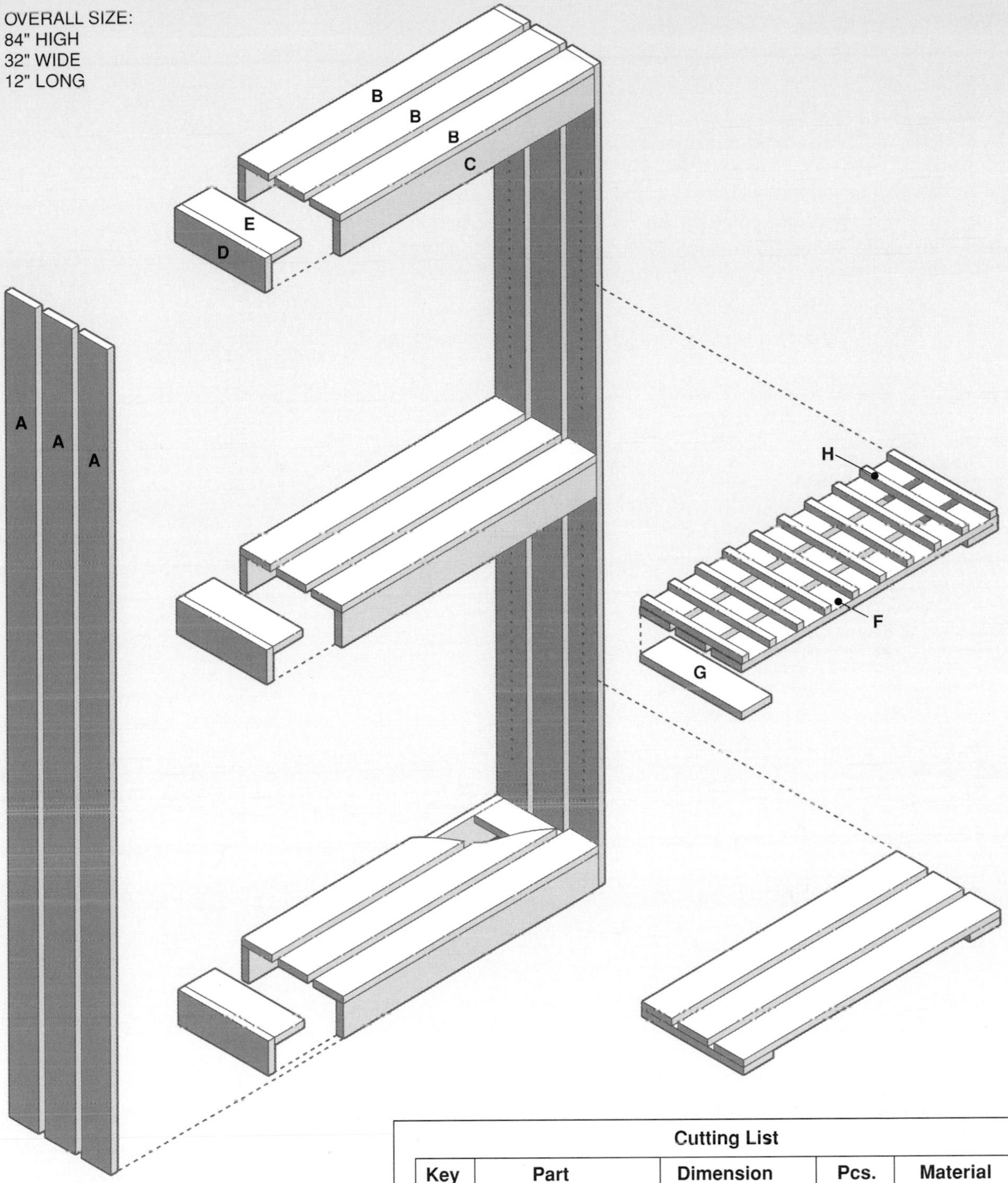
OVERALL SIZE:
84" HIGH
32" WIDE
12" LONG
B
B
B
C
E
D
A
A
A
H
F
G

Cutting List

Key	Part	Dimension	Pcs.	Material
A	Side slats	¾ × 3½ × 84"	6	Pine
B	Fixed-shelf slat	¾ × 3½ × 30½"	9	Pine
C	Fixed-shelf face	¾ × 3½ × 30½"	6	Pine
D	Fixed-shelf end	¾ × 3½ × 10½"	6	Pine
E	Fixed-shelf stretcher	¾ × 3½ × 10½"	6	Pine
F	Adjust.-shelf slat	¾ × 3½ × 30⅜"	6	Pine
G	Adjust.-shelf stretcher	¾ × 3½ × 12"	4	Pine
H	Wine-shelf slat	¾ × ¾ × 12"	10	Pine

Materials: Wood glue, wood screws (#6 × 1¼", #8 × 1⅝"), ¼" shelf pins (8), birch plugs (⅜"), finishing materials.

Note: Measurements reflect the actual thickness of dimensional lumber.

Join the shelf faces to the ends by driving 1⅝" screws through counterbored pilot holes.

Apply glue and drive counterbored screws into the shelf faces and shelf ends to connect the stretchers.

Directions: Pantry Cabinet

MAKE THE FIXED SHELF FRAMES. The fixed shelves comprise the bottom, middle and top of the pantry cabinet. They are essentially box frames that are reinforced internally by stretchers, which in turn help support the three 3½"-wide slats that make up the surface of each shelf. Cut the shelf faces (C), shelf ends (D), and shelf stretchers (E) to size from 1 × 4" pine. Sand the cuts smooth with medium-grit sandpaper. Position the shelf ends between the shelf faces so the corners are flush. Drill ⅜" counterbored pilot holes through the shelf faces into each shelf end. (Keep all counterbores aligned throughout the project to ensure a professional look.) Complete the shelf frame by joining the shelf faces and the shelf ends together with wood glue and 1⅝" wood screws driven through the pilot holes **(photo A).** Repeat for the other two fixed-shelf frames.

ATTACH THE STRETCHERS. Place a stretcher inside the corner of a shelf frame so the stretcher face is flush with the top edges of the frame. Counterbore pilot holes on the shelf faces and ends, and attach the stretcher with glue and 1⅝" screws driven through the pilot holes. Repeat for the other side of the shelf frame and for the other two shelves **(photo B).**

COMPLETE THE FIXED SHELVES. Three slats are fastened to each shelf frame, completing the fixed-shelf units.

Cut the shelf slats (B) to size and sand the edges smooth. Place three slats on your work-surface. Turn one shelf frame over so the stretchers are on the bottom, and place the shelf frame on top of the slats. Move the slats so the corners and

Join the fixed-shelf slats to the stretchers with glue and 1¼"
screws driven through the undersides of the stretchers.

When attaching the side slats, position the outer side slats
so the edge is flush with the edges of the fixed shelves.

edges are flush with the shelf frame. Space the slats ¾" apart and then attach the slats with glue and 1¼" screws countersunk through the bottom of the stretchers into each of the shelf slats **(photo C).** Repeat for the remaining two fixed shelves.

ASSEMBLE THE CABINET. The fixed shelves are connected directly to the side slats to provide stability. The base of the pantry cabinet is wide enough to allow the cabinet to stand alone, so long as the cabinet is square. Make sure all joints are square and the edges are flush during this final assembly.

Cut the side slats (A) to size, and sand to smooth out rough edges. On each side slat, draw a reference line 40" from the bottom end. These lines mark the location of the bottom edge

of the middle fixed shelf. To attach the side slats, align all three shelves on end roughly 40" apart, and lay a side slat over them. Adjust the top and bottom shelves so they are flush with the side slat ends and corners. Adjust the lower edge of the middle shelf so it rests on the reference line. Check that the fixed shelves are correctly aligned and that the corners are square. Counterbore pilot holes through the side slats into the fixed-shelf ends and attach with glue and 1¼" screws.

Position the next side slat flush with the other edge of the fixed shelves, and attach with glue and screws driven through counterbored pilot holes. Center the middle side slat by spacing the slat ¾" between the

outer slats (a scrap of ¾" wood makes a convenient spacer), and attach with glue and screws. With a helper, carefully turn the assembly over so it rests on the attached side slats. Position a side slat over the fixed-shelf ends as before, check to make sure the corners and edges are flush, and attach

TIP

You may find it helpful to clamp workpiece parts during the assembly process. Clamping will hold glued and squared parts securely in place until you permanently fasten them with screws. Large, awkward assemblies are more manageable with the help of a few clamps.

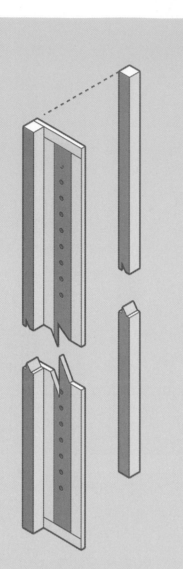

TIP

MAKE A DRILLING TEMPLATE.

Drilling the holes for shelf pegs is simplified by using a template made from a 4 × 34" strip of ⅛ or ¼" pegboard and two 34"-long strips of ¾ × ¾" scrap wood (you can also use stop molding).

First, use masking tape to outline a row of holes on the pegboard. Position one of the ¾" strips against the pegboard so the edge is about 1¾" from the outlined holes. Fasten this guide strip with glue. When the glue dries, turn the template over and attach the second ¾" guide strip, aligning it with the first strip.

Use a pegboard template for uniform placement of peg holes.

the side slat to the fixed shelves **(photo D).** Attach the remaining side slats to the fixed shelves, checking for square as you go.

DRILL THE PEG HOLES. The rows of holes on the inner faces of the side slats are used to hold the pegs for adjustable shelving. Using a drilling template ensures that the holes are perfectly aligned, and the shelves are level when installed *(see Tip).*

Begin by wrapping masking tape around the tip of a ¼" drill bit at a depth of ½". This ensures that you do not drill through the side slats. Next, position the drilling template against the inside face of a side slat with the ¾" guide strip resting against the edge of the slat. Drill a row of peg holes along the inner face of the side slat,

using the pegboard holes as a guide. Make sure not to drill beyond the masking tape depth guide attached to your bit.

Next, rotate the template and position it against the other side slat so the other guide strip is resting against the edge of the slat and the opposite face of the template is facing out. Drill another row of holes exactly parallel to the first row. **(photo E).** When finished drilling, sand the slats to remove any roughness.

MAKE THE ADJUSTABLE SHELVES. Our project includes two adjustable shelves, but you can choose to build more. The adjustable shelves are similar in design to the fixed shelves, but without shelf faces or ends.

For each shelf, cut two stretchers (G) and three slats (F), and sand smooth. Lay three slats on your worksurface. Arrange the stretchers over the ends of the slats so the edges and corners are flush, and the slats are spaced ¾" apart. Drill pilot holes through the stretchers into the slats, and fasten with glue and countersunk 1¼" wood screws.

For wine shelving, the design calls for ten wine slats. Cut the slats (H) to size from ¾" pine, using a circular saw and straightedge guide. (Or, you can use pine stop molding.) Sand the cuts smooth. Place the first slat on the adjustable shelf, ⅛" from one end. Keep the ends of the wine slats even with the edges of the shelf slats, and attach with glue and 4d finish nails. Use a 2½"-wide spacer to guide placement for the rest of the slats, and nail in place. Recess all the nail heads on the wine slats with a nail set as you go **(photo F)**.

APPLY FINISHING TOUCHES. Using a wood mallet, pound glued ⅜"-dia. birch plugs into all counterbored holes **(photo G)**. Carefully sand the plugs flush with a belt sander, and then finish-sand the pantry with fine-grit sandpaper. Wipe the cabinet clean with a rag dipped in mineral spirits. When the wood dries, apply your choice of finish. We brushed a light coat of linseed oil onto the pantry to preserve the natural appearance. If you prefer paint, use a primer and a good-quality enamel. When your finish dries, insert ¼" shelf pins at the desired heights and rest the adjustable shelves on top of the pins.

A 2½"-wide spacer helps ensure uniform placement of the wine shelf cleats.

Use a wood mallet to pound glued ⅜" birch plugs in place.

Car Care Center

*Stash messy car maintenance products
in one compact unit.*

Quantity	Lumber
1	¼" × 2 × 4' hardboard
1	¼" × 2 × 4' tileboard
1	¾" × 4 × 8' ABX plywood
2	1 × 2" × 8' pine
1	1"-dia. × 24" pine dowel

Routine car maintenance is a messy activity involving oil, grime and even hazardous chemicals. Building and using a car care center is a good way to keep the mess of car maintenance concentrated in one spot.

This car care center has a shelf or bin that is designed to accommodate just about any product you put into or onto your car. Included in the design are: an optional sliding shelf for funnels with a shelf for an oil pan below; a tall shelf for anti-freeze and other products sold in tall containers; a towel rod for drying rags; and a separate storage compartment that can be fitted with a locking hasp for potentially hazardous items.

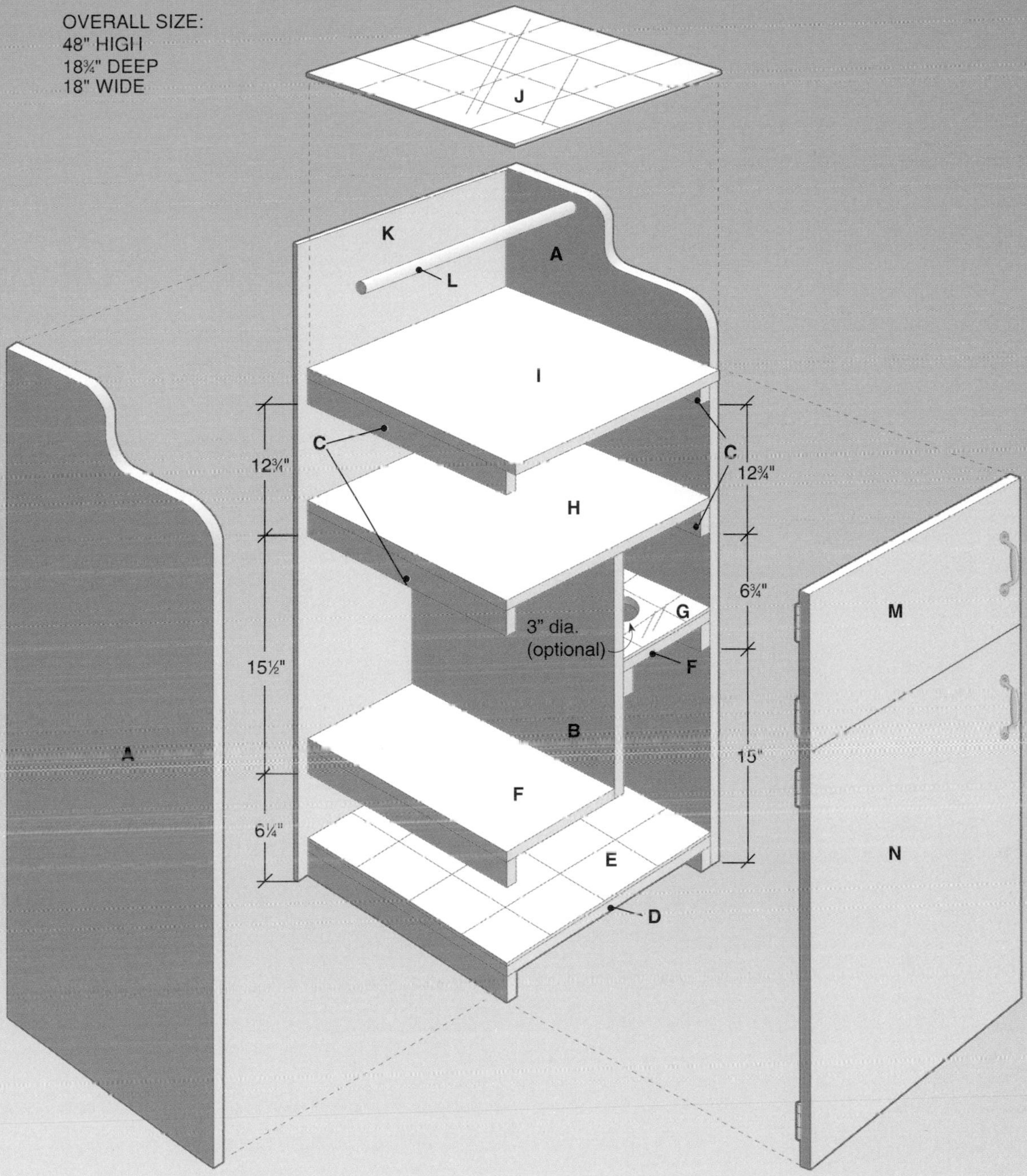
OVERALL SIZE:
48" HIGH
18¾" DEEP
18" WIDE
J
K
L
A
I
C
12¾"
C
12¾"
H
6¾"
G
3" dia.
(optional)
F
15½"
B
F
15"
6¼"
E
D
A
M
N

Cutting List				
Key	**Part**	**Dimension**	**Pcs.**	**Material**
A	Side panel	¾ × 18 × 48"	2	Plywood
B	Center partition	¾ × 18 × 15½"	1	Plywood
C	Cleat	¾ × 1½ × 18"	6	Pine
D	Bottom panel	¾ × 16½ × 18"	1	Plywood
E	Tile cover	¼ × 16½ × 18"	1	Tileboard
F	Bin bottom	¾ × 7⅞ × 18"	2	Plywood
G	Tile cover	¼ × 7⅞ × 18"	1	Tileboard

Cutting List				
Key	**Part**	**Dimension**	**Pcs.**	**Material**
H	Shelf	¾ × 16½ × 18"	1	Plywood
I	Worksurface	¾ × 16½ × 19"	1	Plywood
J	Tile cover	¼ × 16½ × 19"	1	Tileboard
K	Back panel	¼ × 18 × 48"	1	Hardboard
L	Towel rod	1"-dia. × 18"	1	Pine
M	Shelf door	¾ × 18 × 12⅛"	1	Plywood
N	Bin door	¾ × 18 × 23½"	1	Plywood

Materials: Wood glue, #8 × 1¼" wood screws, wood putty, 2 × 2" butt hinges (4), door pulls (2), glide feet (4), and finishing materials.

Note: Measurements reflect the actual size of dimensional lumber.

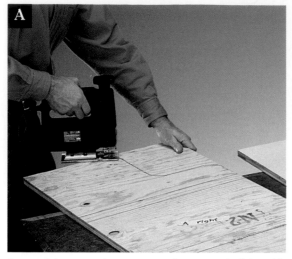

Lay out the curved corners on the top end of the side panel and cut them out with a jig saw.

Mark the shelf cleat positions on the side panels and the center partition, following the spacing shown in the Diagram on page 47.

Directions: Car Care Center

MAKE THE SIDE PANELS, CENTER PARTITION & CLEATS. Cut the side panels (A) for the car care center to size from ¾"-thick plywood. Lay out cutting lines at the top of each side panel: measure 10" from the back, across the top edge, and draw an 8"-long line; measure 9" down the front edge, from the top, and draw a 7"-long line; use a can with a diameter of about 4" to round over the corners where the cutting lines meet, as well as the front edge of the cutout (see *Diagram,* page 93). Cut out the contours with a jig saw **(photo A),** then sand the edges of the cutout until smooth. Use the cutout as a template to draw cutting lines on the second side panel. Next, cut the center partition (B) to size and sand its edges and surfaces. Mark lines across the inside surfaces of side panels at the appropriate cleat locations for each

TIP

Tileboard is a common sheet-goods product, often used in bathrooms for tub and shower surrounds. It is sold in 4 × 8 sheets, in a wide variety of designs and textures.

Fasten the shelf cleats to the side panels and center partition with wood glue and wood screws.

side panel (see *Diagram,* page 93). Transfer the cleat locations to each side of the center partition, using a framing square to make sure the lines are straight and perpendicular to the edges of the panels **(photo B).** Make sure the bottoms of the partition and the side panel are aligned. Cut the shelf cleats (C) from 1 × 2 pine and attach them to the side panels and center partition at the marked locations, using wood glue and counterbored #6 × 1¼" wood screws **(photo C).**

ASSEMBLE THE SHELVES & SIDE PANELS. Cut the bottom panel (D), bin bottoms (F) and shelf (H). Stand the side panels upright and place the bottom panel on the bottom cleats. Fasten the bottom panel to the cleats with glue and screws. Cut a 6¼"-long spacer and stand it on the bottom panel to support the lower bin bottom while you attach it to the cleat on the left side panel. Then, fasten the center partition to the bin bottom, keeping the bottom edges flush, with glue and screws driven through the partition and into the edge of the bin bottom. Use at least three screws. Set the upper bin bottom onto the cleats. If you use funnels to change the fluid in your car, do not attach this shelf permanently. Then, after you attach the tile cover, cut out a 3"-dia. hole in the center to hold funnels. Simply slide out the shelf to insert the funnel—be sure to place an oil pan below to catch the drips. But if you do not use funnels, go ahead and attach the bin bottom to the cleats, and don't bother cutting the hole in the center. Attach the full-width shelf (H) to the cleats on the side panels, then drive two or three screws through the shelf and down into the top edge of the partition **(photo D)**. Cut the worksurface (I) and attach it to the top cleats.

INSTALL THE TILE COVERS. Cut tile covers (E, G, J) from a sheet of ⅛"-thick tileboard. Fasten them to the bottom panel, lower bin bottom, and worksurface, respectively. Use panel adhesive or tileboard adhesive to attach the tileboard **(photo E).** Set the tileboard by rolling it with an old rolling pin or a J-roller. If you plan to use the upper bin bottom for a funnel, cut a 3"-dia. hole in the center.

ATTACH THE DOORS & BACK PANEL. Cut the back (K) to size from ¼"-thick hardboard and fasten in place with 1" wire nails driven into the back edges of the cabinet. Cut the shelf door (M) and bin door (N). Attach two utility hinges to each door and hang the doors, making sure the space between the doors falls over the front edge of the full-width shelf.

APPLY FINISHING TOUCHES. Cut a 1"-dia. dowel to 18" in length to use as a towel rod (L). Drill 1"-dia holes for the dowel in the side panels, 2" down from the top edge and 5" in from the back on each panel. Insert the rod through the holes so the ends are flush with the outside surfaces of the panels. Pull the rod out slightly and apply glue to the ends, then reinsert the ends into the holes. Tack glide feet to the underside of the bottom panel. Fill screw counterbores and exposed plywood edges with wood putty, then sand all surfaces smooth. Apply paint or a protective topcoat. Attach a door pull to each door, and add a locking hasp to the cabinet door if desired.

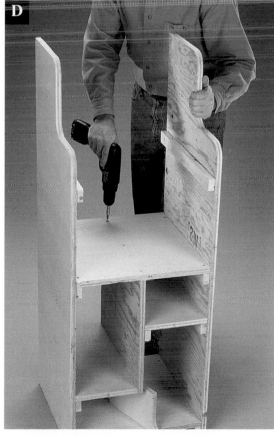

Attach the full-width shelf to the partition.

Cover surfaces with tileboard for easy cleanup.

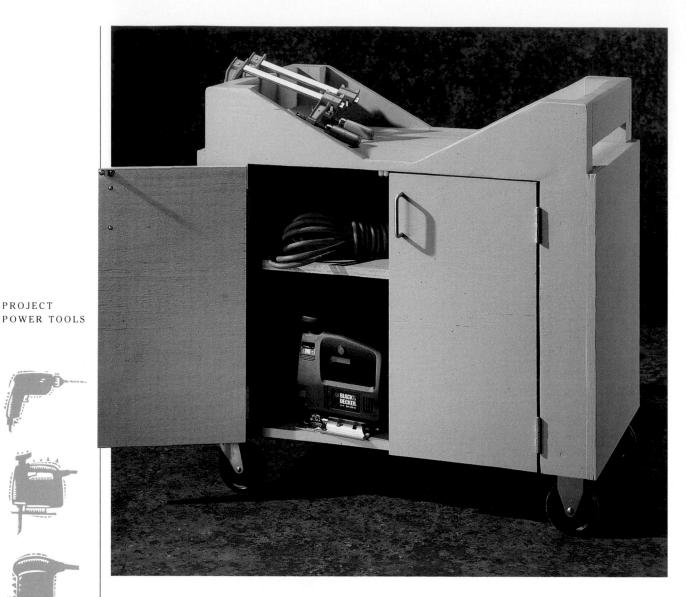

Rolling Tool Cart

*Part storage cabinet, part sawhorse, the tool locker allows you to
wheel your tools right to the job site.*

Put a stop to those endless tool-fetching trips from your garage to your work site with this rolling tool cart. Big enough to hold all the tools you'll need for just

about any job or project, the rolling tool cart also doubles as a sturdy worksurface. The cutouts on the top create clearance for long boards, and the four corners of the top give ample support to full-size sheet goods. When you're not using the top as a worksurface, the ends make a convenient holding area for clamps. With four sturdy casters and cabinet doors that snap shut securely,

this tool cart can be rolled along almost any surface without sending your valuable hand tools and portable power tools clattering to the ground. The rolling tool cart is made by attaching plywood panels to a 2 × 4 pine frame. With a little ingenuity and planning, all the plywood parts for this project can be cut from a single sheet of ¾"-thick plywood.

CONSTRUCTION MATERIALS

Quantity	Lumber
1	¾" × 4 × 8' plywood
3	2 × 4" × 8' pine

96

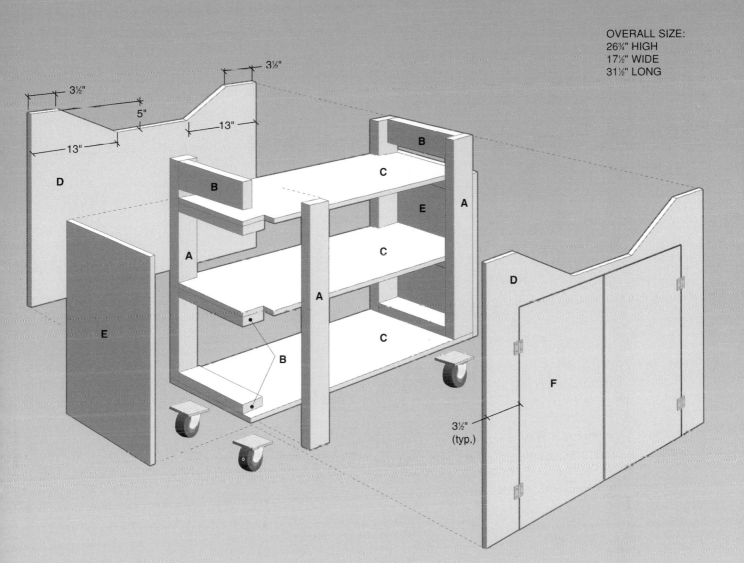

OVERALL SIZE:
26¾" HIGH
17½" WIDE
31½" LONG

3½"

3½"

5"

13"

13"

B

D

A

C

E

A

B

A

C

B

A

C

D

F

3½"
(typ.)

Cutting List				
Key	**Part**	**Dimension**	**Pcs.**	**Material**
A	Post	1½ × 3½ × 26"	4	Pine
B	Rail	1½ × 3½ × 13"	8	Pine
C	Shelf	¾ × 16 × 30"	3	Plywood

Cutting List				
Key	**Part**	**Dimension**	**Pcs.**	**Material**
D	Front, back	¾ × 30 × 26¾"	2	Plywood
E	End panel	¾ × 17½ × 21¾"	2	Plywood
F	Door	¾ × 11¾₆ × 20¾"	2	Plywood

Materials: Glue, 1½ × 3" butt hinges (4), double roller catches (2), 3"-dia. locking casters (4), wood screws (#6 × 2", #6 × 2½"), finishing materials.

Specialty Items: Straightedge guide, bar clamps, tape measure.

Note: Measurements reflect the actual size of dimensional lumber.

Fasten the rail between the posts with glue and wood screws.

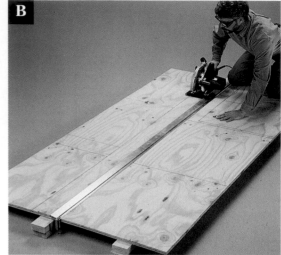

Cut the cabinet shelves from a sheet of plywood, using a circular saw and straightedge guide.

Directions: Rolling Tool Cart

BUILD THE CABINET FRAMES. The rails are attached between sets of posts to form two frames that are the structural anchors for the project. Start by cutting the posts (A) and rails (B) to size. Sand these and all parts with medium-grit sandpaper after cutting. Clamp one rail between two posts ends, making sure their edges are flush. Fasten the pieces with glue and #6 × 2½" wood screws **(photo A).** Repeat this procedure with another rail-and-post pair. Mark reference lines for shelf locations 12" up from one end of the posts and 5¾" from the other end, across their inside faces. Position the rails on the reference lines so their top faces are on these lines, and fasten them with glue and wood screws. Fasten the top

Draw cutting lines for the front and back panels according to the Diagram on page 97.

rails between the posts with the top edges flush with the tops of the posts. The outside faces of these top rails should be flush with the outsides of the posts.

INSTALL SHELVES BETWEEN THE CABINET FRAMES. The rolling tool cart has a bottom shelf, a middle shelf, and a top worksurface. The middle shelf and the worksurface are notched at their corners to fit around the 2 × 4 posts. Cut the shelves (C) to size from ¾"-thick plywood **(photo B),** then cut 3½ × 1½" notches in the corners of two of the

shelves (see *Diagram*, page 97) so they fit around the posts. Use a jig saw to cut the corner notches. Attach the shelf without notches to the bottom ends of the cabinet frames. Make sure the ends with the higher shelf rails are joined to the base, flush with the ends. Use glue and #6 × 2" wood screws driven up through the base and into the bottom ends of the frames. Attach the notched shelves to the middle and upper sets of rails, using glue and screws.

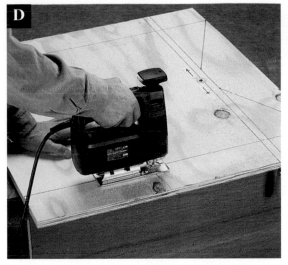

Use a jig saw to cut a 21 × 23" rectangle from the front face panel.

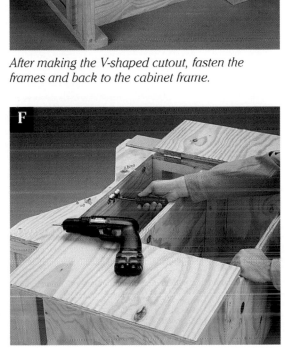

After making the V-shaped cutout, fasten the frames and back to the cabinet frame.

MAKE THE FRONT & BACK. The front and back parts of the cabinet start out the same size and shape, but the front panel is cut out in the center to make a face frame for the cabinet doors (which are made from the cutout plywood). Cut two pieces of plywood to size for the front and back (D). Mark cutting lines for the V-shaped cutout at the top of each piece (see *Diagram*, page 97). On one of the panels (this will be the front), draw cutting lines for the door cutout 3½" in from the sides and ¾" down from the bottom of the V-shaped cutout. This will create a cutout that is 23" wide and 21" high **(photo C).** Make the V-shaped cutouts in both workpieces with a jig saw, then sand the parts smooth. Make the door cutout on the front panel by cutting along the guidelines with a jig saw, forming a 23 × 21" rectangle **(photo D).** Cut carefully—the waste piece can be cut down the center to create the cabinet doors (F). Use glue and #6 × 2" wood screws to attach the panels at the front and back **(photo E).** Save the cutout rectangle to make the doors (F).

MAKE THE ENDS. The ends (E) are same-sized plywood panels that are attached along the sides of the rolling tool cart. Cut the two panels to size, and use glue and #6 × 2" wood screws to attach the end panels with their top edges flush with the top shelf.

INSTALL THE DOORS. The cabinet doors are made from a 23 × 21"-high piece of plywood. If possible, use the cutout from the front panel. Use a circular saw to cut the doors to size. Sand their edges with a belt sander mounted on your worksurface, and attach them to the front panel with evenly spaced 1½ × 3" butt hinges, making sure to maintain a ¼"-wide gap between the panel frame and the door edges and a ⅛"-wide gap between the doors.

APPLY FINISHING TOUCHES. Attach door handles and double roller door catches **(photo F),** and attach heavy-duty, 3" locking casters on the bottom of the posts. Make sure to center the casters on the posts to enable the tool cart to roll easily and smoothly. Locking casters are necessary if you want a stable workstation. Paint the project inside and out with a hard enamel paint.

Attach the door catches, handles and casters to the rolling tool cart.

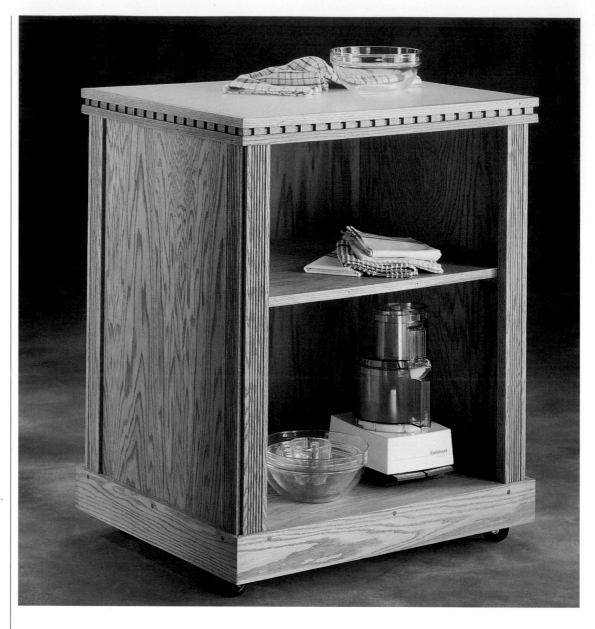

Utility Cart

Form and function combine in this richly detailed rolling cart.

CONSTRUCTION MATERIALS

Quantity	Lumber
2	1 × 2" × 6' oak
2	1 × 4" × 6' oak
1	2 × 4" × 4' pine
1	1 × 4" × 6' pine
1	¾" × 4 × 8' oak plywood
2	⅜ × ⅝" × 6' dentil molding
4	¾ × ¾" × 6' stop molding
8	⅜ × 2¼" × 3' beaded casing
4	¾" × 2 × 3' melamine-coated particleboard

You'll appreciate the extra space, and your guests will admire the classic style of this movable cabinet. The cart features decorative dentil molding around a scratch-resistant 22 × 28½" countertop that provides additional work-surface space for preparing special dishes. Two storage or display areas, framed by banded corner moldings, can hold food, beverages, dinnerware and appliances. Underneath, the cart has casters so it easily rolls across floors to the preparing or serving area. Time and again, you'll find this versatile cart a great help in the kitchen, dining room or other entertainment areas of your home.

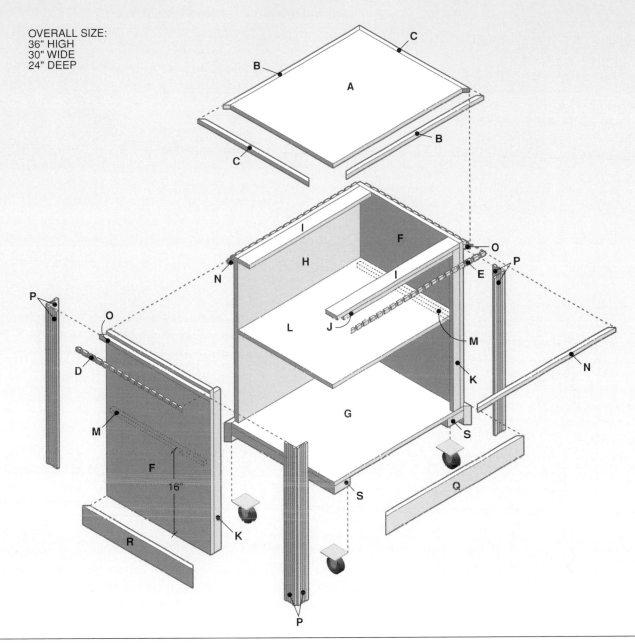

OVERALL SIZE:
36" HIGH
30" WIDE
24" DEEP

16"

Cutting List

Key	Part	Dimension	Pcs.	Material
A	Top	¾ × 22½ × 28½"	1	Particleboard
B	Long upper trim	¾ × ¾ × 30"	2	Stop mld.
C	Short upper trim	¾ × ¾ × 24"	2	Stop mld.
D	Short dentil	⅜ × ⅝ × 23¼"	2	Dentil mld.
E	Long dentil	⅜ × ⅝ × 29¼"	2	Dentil mld.
F	Side panel	¾ × 22½ × 30⅞"	2	Plywood
G	Bottom	¾ × 22½ × 28½"	1	Plywood
H	Back	¾ × 27 × 30⅞"	1	Plywood
I	Stretcher	¾ × 3½ × 27"	2	Pine
J	Brace	¾ × 1½ × 24"	1	Oak

Cutting List

Key	Part	Dimension	Pcs.	Material
K	Post	¾ × 1½ × 30⅛"	2	Oak
L	Shelf	¾ × 20¾ × 27"	1	Plywood
M	Cleat	¾ × ¾ × 20¼ "	2	Stop mld.
N	Long lower trim	¾ × ¾ × 30"	2	Stop mld.
O	Short lower trim	¾ × ¾ × 24"	2	Stop mld.
P	Corner trim	⅜ × 2¼ × 29½"	8	Bead. csg.
Q	Long base	¾ × 3½ × 30"	2	Oak
R	Short base	¾ × 3½ × 24"	2	Oak
S	Caster mount	1½ × 3½ × 22½"	2	Pine

Materials: Wood glue, #6 wood screws (1¼", 1⅝", 2"), 4d finish nails, 16-ga. brads, shelf nosing or oak veneer edge tape (30"), 2" casters (4), finishing materials.

Note: Measurements reflect the actual thickness of dimensional lumber.

Use a ¾" piece of scrap wood as a spacer to ensure that the cleats are inset ¾" from the edges of the side panels.

Drive screws through the top of the stretcher to secure the oak brace.

Directions: Utility Cart

PREPARE THE SIDES AND BOTTOM. Pilot holes are predrilled into the side panels to make attaching the back and posts easier, and cleats are attached to support the shelf. Start by cutting the side panels (F), bottom (G), back (H) and cleats (M) to size, and sand smooth. Drill four evenly spaced countersunk pilot holes along the long edges of each side panel, ⅜" in from each edge. (Draw a light reference line to help you align the pilot holes.) Flip each side over and, on the inside face, place the cleat so the bottom edge is 16" from the bottom of the side panel. Drill pilot holes and attach the cleat using glue and 1¼" screws. Make sure the

ends of the cleats are inset ¾" from the edges of the side panel **(photo A).** Drill countersunk pilot holes along the side and back edges of the bottom as well, but leave the front edge intact.

ASSEMBLE THE CART. Position the back between the side panels, and attach with glue and 1⅝" screws driven through the pilot holes into the back. Attach the bottom panel with glue and screws. Next, cut the stretchers (I), brace (J), posts (K) and shelf (L) to size. Place the stretchers across the top of the cart so the tops are flush at the corners, and attach with glue and 1⅝" screws. Drive screws through the back into the rear stretcher as well. Set the posts in place, faces flush against the side edges, and at-

tach with glue and screws driven through the pilot holes in the sides. Apply glue to the brace, and clamp it to the front stretcher. Drive 1¼" screws through the stretcher into the brace **(photo B).** Clamp the shelf vertically to your worksurface. Cut a strip of shelf nosing to match the length of the front edge, apply glue and attach to the shelf. Use wire brads to secure the nosing in place **(photo C).** Apply glue to the tops of the cleats, and set the shelf into position inside the cart. Drill pilot holes and nail 4d finish nails through the shelf into the cleats.

ATTACH THE UPPER MOLDING. A series of moldings are fastened to the top of the cart, providing a finished look. A miter box and backsaw (or a power

Use glue and brads to attach the shelf nosing in place.

Secure the molding in place with 1" finish nails.

miter box) are useful tools for making the 45° cuts. If you do not have access to a miter box, carefully make the cuts with a jig saw or coping saw. Cut the short dentils (D), long dentils (E), long lower trim pieces (N) and short lower trim pieces (O) to length. Make 45° cuts in the ends of each piece of molding, always angling the cuts inward. When cutting the miters for the dentil molding, make sure to cut through the blocks, or "teeth" of each molding piece so the repeat pattern will match at the corners. Due to variations in dentil molding, you may want to buy extra molding so your pieces align properly. When you've cut the molding, fit the dentil pieces, with the gap edge up, flush to the top edge of the cart. Drill pi-

lot holes for 16-ga. brads, then attach the molding with glue and brads **(photo D).**
Attach the lower trim pieces below the dentil molding with brads, and recess all nail heads with a nail set **(photo E).**

ATTACH THE BASE MOLDING. Cut the corner trim (P), long bases (Q), short bases (R) and caster mounts (S) to size. Lay the cart on its back and attach the caster mounts to the bottom of the cart, flush with the bottom edges, using glue and 2" screws. Miter-cut the base pieces, and drill counterbored

pilot holes through the upper part of each base piece. Attach the base pieces with glue and 1¼" screws, making sure the tops of the base pieces are flush with the top edge of the bottom. Apply glue to a corner trim piece and clamp in place over a post so the edges are flush **(photo F).** Drill pilot holes, and secure with finish nails. When the glue is dry, complete the corner by attaching another trim piece with glue and finish nails. The edge of the trim pieces should just touch, but should not overlap. Do this

OPTION

Instead of fastening shelf nosing to the shelf edge, an option is to apply iron-on oak veneer edge tape. Cut the tape to length, and use a household iron to activate the adhesive. When cool, trim away excess tape with a sharp utility knife.

for all four corners, and recess all nail heads with a nail set.

MAKE THE TOP. Mark the dimensions for the top (A) on a piece of melamine-coated particleboard. Apply masking tape over the cut lines, and score them using a straightedge and utility knife **(photo G).** To minimize chip-out when making the cut, use a new or very sharp blade on your circular saw. Cut the top to size, and remove the masking tape. Cut the long upper trim pieces (B) and short upper trim pieces (C) to length, mitering the ends at 45°. Drill pilot holes, and attach the trim pieces with glue and finish nails. Align and center the top over the utility cart, and attach the top with glue and 1¼" screws driven up through the stretchers and into the underside of the top **(photo H).**

APPLY FINISHING TOUCHES. Lay the utility cart on its back, and install the casters. Apply wood putty to all recessed nail heads, and fill the counterbores on the base trim with glued wood plugs. Sand the cabinet smooth, and finish with a stain or sealer of your choice. We used a rustic oak stain to enhance the natural wood appeal.

E

Attach lower trim underneath the dentil molding, and recess nail heads with a nail set.

F

Clamp the corner molding in place to ensure a tight bond with the posts.

Score the cut lines on the melamine with a utility knife to make saw-ing easier.

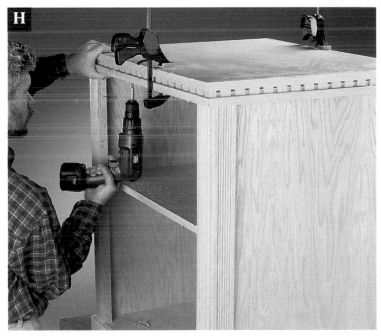

Apply glue and clamp the top in place, and secure with screws driven through the brace and stretchers.

TIP

The size of the teeth in dentil molding can vary, as can the gaps between teeth. You might want to purchase extra molding so you can adjust when cutting to get the corners to come out properly.

Pet Supply Center

Store pet equipment, medicine and food in this all-in-one storage center with a built-in pet food dispenser.

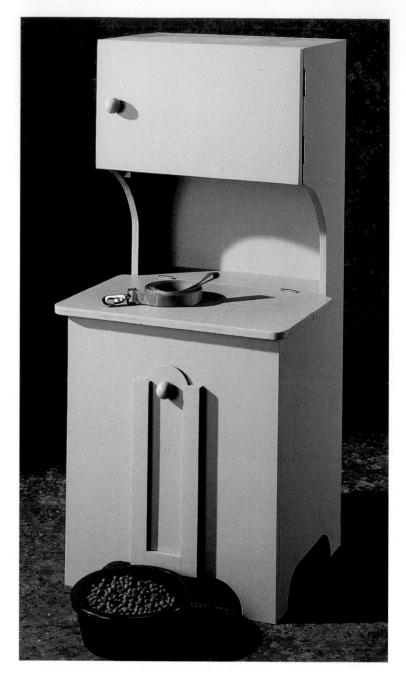

Most pet owners know that keeping track of all of the necessary equipment and supplies your pet needs can sometimes get a little overwhelming. With this uniquely designed pet supply center, you can keep all the necessary items for your pet in one central unit. In addition, this storage center has a built-in pet food bin and dispenser to eliminate wrestling with bulky and messy pet food bags and scoops every time your pet's dinner bell rings. Simply place the pet's dish below the dispenser opening and raise the hopper until the bowl is full.

The bi-fold lid can be used as a countertop, but it also flips up easily to make loading pet food into the bin easy. The upper cabinet is a suitable place for just about any pet things you need to store, such as cans of pet food, medicine, grooming equipment, pet food and water dishes, or leashes and collars. Built mostly from plywood, the pet supply center can be finished so it fits into just about any area of your house.

CONSTRUCTION MATERIALS

Quantity	Lumber
1	¼" × 2 × 4' hardboard
1	⅜" × 2 × 4' AC plywood
1	¾" × 4 × 8' AC plywood
2	1 × 2" × 8' pine

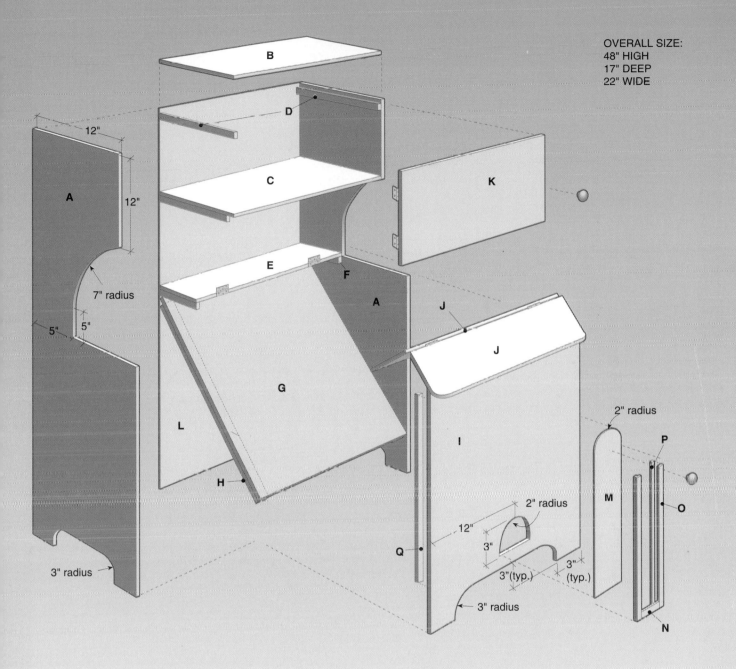

OVERALL SIZE:
48" HIGH
17" DEEP
22" WIDE

Cutting List				
Key	Part	Dimension	Pcs.	Material
A	Side panel	¾ × 17 × 48"	2	Plywood
B	Top panel	¾ × 12 × 18½"	1	Plywood
C	Cabinet shelf	¾ × 12 × 18½"	1	Plywood
D	Cabinet cleat	¾ × 1½ × 12"	4	Pine
E	Lid support	¾ × 5 × 18½"	1	Plywood
F	Lid cleat	¾ × 1½ × 17"	2	Pine
G	Bin tray	¾ × 18½ × 24"	1	Plywood
H	Bin tray cleat	¾ × 1½ × 21"	2	Pine
I	Front panel	¾ × 20 × 24"	1	Plywood

Cutting List				
Key	Part	Dimension	Pcs.	Material
J	Lid half	¾ × 22 × 7"	2	Plywood
K	Cabinet door	¾ × 12 × 20"	1	Plywood
L	Back panel	¼ × 20 × 48"	1	Hardboard
M	Hopper door	¼ × 4 × 16"	1	Hardboard
N	Door stop	¾ × 1½ × 13½"	1	Pine
O	Door track (front)	⅜ × 1¼ × 12"	2	Plywood
P	Door track (back)	⅜ × 1 × 12"	2	Plywood
Q	Corner cleat	¾ × 1½ × 18"	2	Pine

Materials: Wood glue, #6 × 1¼" wood screws, 2d common nails, (6) 2 × 2" butt hinges, drawer knob, finishing materials.

Note: Measurements reflect the actual size of dimensional lumber.

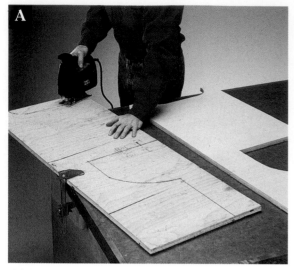

Make the curved cutouts in the side panels using a jig saw.

Mark the cleat positions on the side panel, using a framing square to make sure the lines are perpendicular to the sides of the panels.

Directions:
Pet Supply Center

MAKE THE SIDE PANELS. Start by cutting the side panels (A) to size from ¾" plywood, using a circular saw and straightedge cutting guide. Draw cutting lines onto one side panel for the flat-topped arc that is cut in the bottom to create the feet, and for the quarter-round recess that is cut out level with the top of the food bin. The *Diagram* on page 107 contains all the cutting information you'll need to plot and cut these shapes. Use a jig saw to cut out the bottom arc and the lid recess. Sand both cutouts smooth, then use the side panel as a template to mark the other side panel. Cut and sand the second panel **(photo A).**

MAKE & ATTACH THE CLEATS. The shelves in the cabinet area, the bi-fold lid and lid support, and the tray in the food bin are supported by cleats mounted on the inside faces of the side panels. Cleats also are used at the joints between the front panel and the side panels. Cut the cabinet cleats (D), the lid

Fasten the shelf cleats and tray cleats to the side panels at their marked positions using wood glue and screws.

cleats (F), the bin tray cleats (H) and the corner cleats (Q) from 1 × 2 pine. Mark the position of the lid cleats on the side panels so they are flush with the straight bottoms of the recess cutouts (see *Diagram,* page 107). To lay out the locations for the bin tray cleats, draw a diagonal line on each side panel, starting 3¾" up from the bottom at the front edge, and running to the bottom of the lid cleat location, where it meets the back edge of the side panel. This line marks the position for the bottom of the ¾"-

thick bin tray. Draw a second diagonal line on each panel, parallel to the first and 1½" below it to mark the bottom edge of the bin tray cleat on each panel. Lay out the top and bottom locations for the cabinet cleats on the inside surfaces of the side panels **(photo B).** One pair of cleats should be flush with the tops of the panels, and the bottoms of the other pair should be 12" down from the tops of the panels. Use a framing square to make sure these lines are perpendicular to the sides of the panels. Attach

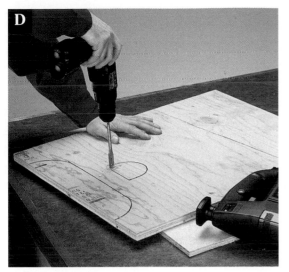

Drill a starter hole, then cut the dispenser opening with a jig saw.

cleats at the lines with glue and #6 × 1¼" wood screws **(photo C).** You may need to trim the ends of the lower cabinet cleats or the bin tray cleats so they do not stick out past the edges of the side panels. Finally, attach the corner cleats flush with the front edges of the side panels, centered between the bin tray cleats and the lid cleats.

ATTACH THE TOP, SHELF, LID SUPPORT & TRAY. Cut the top (B), cabinet shelf (C), lid support (E), and bin tray (G). Sand the surfaces and edges of all pieces with medium-grit sandpaper and a power sander. Prop the side panels up with the inside faces facing one another. Glue and screw the top, cabinet shelf, lid supports and tray to the appropriate cleats on the side panels. Make sure the front and back edges of the parts are flush with the front and back edges of the side panels.

MAKE & ATTACH THE FRONT PANEL. Cut the front panel (I) to size from ¾"-thick plywood. Draw cutout shapes for the flat-topped arc at the bottom of the panel, and the bin dispenser hole, according to the dimensions in the *Diagram* on page 107. Drill a starter hole inside the dispenser hole cutout **(photo D),** then make both cutouts with a jig saw and sand the edges smooth. Attach the front panel to the corner cleats at the front edges of the side panels.

ATTACH THE LID & CABINET DOOR. The lid for the bin is made of two pieces of plywood hinged together so they open like a bi-fold door. Cut the lid halves (J) and the cabinet door (K). Use a jig saw to round over the front corners of the front half of the lid to about a 1" radius. Press the square edge of the front half against an edge of the back half of the lid, and join them together with two 2 × 2" butt hinges mounted on the undersides of the lid halves. Mount the lid assembly to the lid support with two 2 × 2" butt hinges **(photo E).** Attach the cabinet door to the side panel with two 2 × 2" butt hinges.

INSTALL THE HOPPER DOOR. The hopper door slides up and down over the dispenser hole to let pet food flow out of the bin. Cut the hopper door (M), the door stop (N), and the front and back door tracks (O, P). Use a compass set to a 2" radius to draw a roundover cutting line at the top of the hopper door, and cut the roundover with a jig saw. Attach a drawer knob to the hopper door. The door is fitted inside tracks so it can slide up and down. Attach the door stop to the front panel with glue and screws, flush with the bottom edge of the dispenser hole on the front panel. Attach the back door tracks to the front panel in a vertical position, ¼" away from each end of the stop and flush with the arc cutout. Tack the front door tracks on top of the back tracks so their outside edges are flush. Insert the hopper door inside the tracks.

APPLY FINISHING TOUCHES. Cut the back panel (L) and fasten it to the back of the unit with 2d common nails. Fill screw counterbores and exposed plywood edges with wood putty, then sand all surfaces smooth. Apply your finish of choice (we used enamel paint).

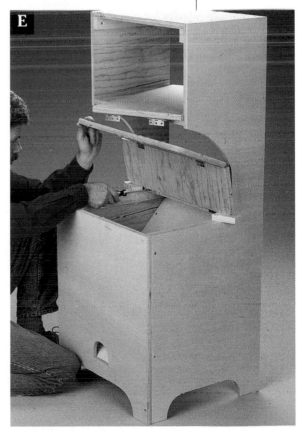

Mount the hinged, bi-fold lid to the lid support with butt hinges.

Recycling Center

Recycling is no longer a chore when this convenient recycling center is a fixture in your kitchen.

CONSTRUCTION MATERIALS

Quantity	Lumber
1	¾" × 4 × 8' birch plywood
1	1¼"-dia. × 36" birch dowel
3	¼ × 3 × 3" Masonite® or scrap wood

Finding adequate storage for recyclables in a kitchen or pantry is a real challenge. Gaping paper bags of discarded aluminum, newspaper, glass and plastic look awful and can be a real nuisance. Our recycling center eliminates the nuisance and makes recycling easy. The recycling center holds up to four bags of recyclables, keeping the materials in one place and out of sight. Arches on the bottom of the cabinet create the four feet and are echoed on the front edges. The two spacious bins pivot forward on a dowel for easy deposit and removal of recyclables, and the top of the cabinet is sturdy enough to serve as a shelf.

110

OVERALL SIZE:
23³/₄" HIGH
34³/₄" WIDE
14³/₄" DEEP

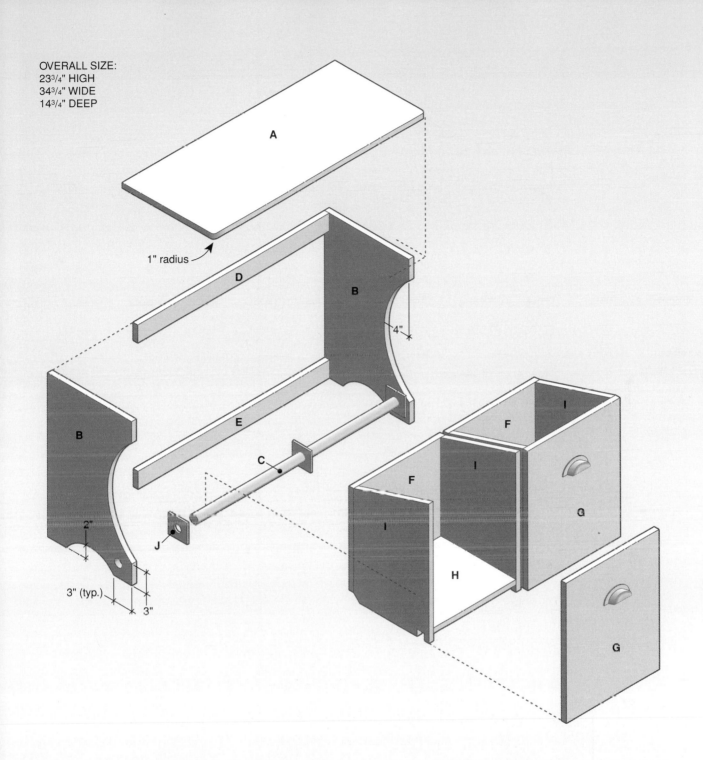

1" radius

4"

2"

3" (typ.)

3"

Key	Part	Dimension	Pcs.	Material
Cutting List				
A	Top	¾ × 14¾ × 34¾"	1	Plywood
B	End	¾ × 13¾ × 23"	2	Plywood
C	Dowel	1¼"-dia. × 34"	1	Birch dowel
D	Top stretcher	¾ × 2½ × 31"	1	Plywood
E	Bottom stretcher	¾ × 2½ × 31"	1	Plywood

Key	Part	Dimension	Pcs.	Material
Cutting List				
F	Bin back	¾ × 15 × 16½"	2	Plywood
G	Bin front	¾ × 15 × 19½"	2	Plywood
H	Bin bottom	¾ × 12¼ × 13½"	2	Plywood
I	Bin side	¾ × 12¼ × 19½"	4	Plywood
J	Spacer	¼ × 3 × 3"	3	Masonite

Materials: Wood glue, wood screws (#6 × 1½", #8 × 2", #4 × ⅜"), 4d finish nails, 10" metal chains (2), drawer pulls (2), paste wax, finishing materials.
Note: Measurements reflect the actual thickness of dimensional lumber.

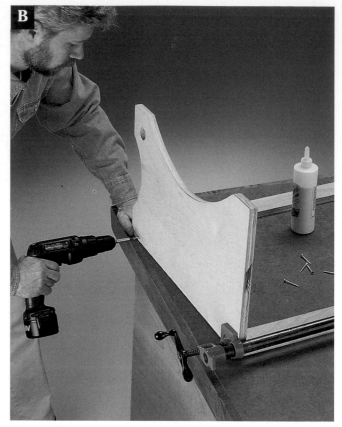

Drill countersunk pilot holes through the bottom edges into the dowel holes.

Glue and drill screws through the frame sides into the stretchers. Use bar clamps to ensure square joints.

Directions: Recycling Center

MAKE THE TOPS AND ENDS. The ends have arches on the bottoms to create the four feet and longer decorative arches on the sides.

Cut the top (A) and ends (B) to size from plywood, and sand the edges smooth with medium-grit sandpaper. To create rounded front corners on the top, use a compass set for 1", and draw the roundovers. Sand the corners down to the curves with a belt sander.

An easy way to draw the arches on the end pieces is to use a thin, flexible piece of metal, plastic or wood as a tracing guide. Along the front edge of each side, make marks 3" in from each corner. Make another mark 4" up from the centerpoint of the front edge. Tack casing nails at these three points. Hook the flexible guide over the center nail, then flex each end to the nails so the strip bows out to create a smooth curve. Trace the arches and remove the casing nails. Draw the curves for the bottom

edges, using the same technique. Along the bottom edges, measure 3" in from the bottom corners and 2" up from the centerpoint of the bottom edge. Tack casing nails at the marks, hook the guide and trace the arches. Make the cuts for the bottom and front arches with a jig saw, and sand smooth with medium-grit sandpaper.

Mark the dowel hole locations on each end piece, 2¼" in and 2" up from the bottom front corner. Use a 1¼" spade bit to drill the dowel holes. Drill countersunk pilot holes for the anchor screws along the bottom edge **(photo A).**

TIP

When checking a cabinet for square, measure diagonally from corner to corner. If the measurements are equal, the cabinet is square. Apply pressure to one side or the other with your hand or clamps to push a cabinet back into square.

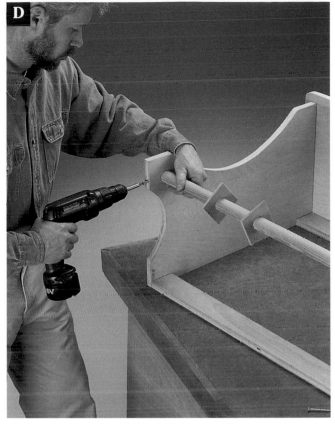

Draw reference lines on the top to help center in place when attaching the top to the sides.

Anchor the dowel by driving #8 x 2" wood screws through the predrilled holes into the dowel.

ASSEMBLE THE CABINET FRAME. The top and bottom stretchers form the back of the unit and provide much of its stability.

Cut the dowel (C), the top stretcher (D) and the bottom stretcher (E) to size, and sand smooth. Position the stretchers between the sides so they are flush at the edges and corners, and clamp in place with bar clamps. Drill countersunk pilot holes, then attach the end pieces to the stretchers with glue and 1½" wood screws **(photo B).**

With the cabinet lying on its back, position the top piece bottom-side-up against the top stretcher, so the edges overlap evenly. Mark the bottom surface of the top piece to indicate where it will rest on the cabinet ends **(photo C).** Set the cabinet upright and position the top, aligning it with the reference lines. Drill pilot holes, and attach the top to the ends and top stretcher with glue and 1½" screws.

INSERT THE DOWEL. Spacers are placed on the dowel to separate the bins and to give the unit a smooth opening and closing action.

Make the three spacers (J) by cutting 3" squares out of scrap

TIP

Careful planning can prevent valuable wood from being wasted. With the exception of the dowel and the spacers, all the parts for this project can be cut from a 4 × 8' piece of birch plywood (see pattern below):

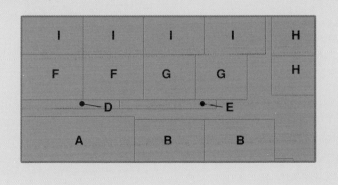

Clamp the bin sides to your worksurface and use a jig saw to cut the notches and bevels.

Position the bin bottom flush with the dowel notch and attach with glue and screws.

¼" material, such as Masonite. Next, locate the centerpoints of the spacers and drill out holes with a 1¼" spade bit to accommodate the dowel. Apply paste wax to the dowel for lubrication. Slide the dowel through one end piece, then through the spacers, and finally through the other end. Position the dowel so it extends out evenly on both sides. Fix the dowel in position by driving 2" wood screws through the pilot holes on the bottom edges of the ends and into the dowel **(photo D).**

MAKE THE BIN SIDES. The bin sides have a notch near the bottom front edge so they can rock safely on the dowel. There are bevels on the top edge and at bottom rear corners to provide clearance.

Cut the bin sides (I) to size, and sand smooth. Use a jig saw to cut a 1¼"-wide, 1"-high notch, located ¾" from the bottom front corner of each bin side (*see Detail,* opposite page). For the short bevel on the bottom, measure and make marks 1" from the bottom rear corner. Draw a cut line between these two marks, and cut off the 1 × 1" corner with a jig saw. For the long bevel on the top edge, measure 2" down from the top back corner and make a mark.

With a straightedge, draw a cut line from the mark to the upper front corner and make the cut with a jig saw **(photo E).** Sand all cuts smooth.

ASSEMBLE THE BINS. The bins are designed to fit underneath the cabinet top. Make sure that all cuts and joints are square so the bins fit properly.

Cut the bin back (F), bin front (G) and bin bottom (H) to size, and sand smooth. Position the sides and front so the edges are flush, then drill coun-

TIP

Using a combination square as a marking gauge is much more convenient than making a series of measured points and connecting them with a straightedge. If you need to scribe a line, just set the combination square to your desired dimension, hold pencil and slide square along workpiece, marking as you go.

tersunk pilot holes and attach the bin front to the bin sides with glue and 1½" screws. Position the bin bottom between the sides so it is recessed 1" and is flush with the top of the dowel notches. Drill countersunk pilot holes, and attach the sides and back to the bottom with glue and 1½" screws **(photo F).** Position the bin back so the top edge is flush with the top of the bin. Drill countersunk pilot holes, and attach the back with glue and 1½" screws.

ATTACH THE CHAIN. To prevent the bins from falling forward when adding or removing recyclables, our design uses chain to attach the bins to the top. The chains can be easily detached from eye hooks when cleaning needs to be done.

Center and attach the open eye hooks on the top edge of the bin backs. Attach 10" chains with ⅜" screws to the underside of the top, 8" from the front edge and 8" from the sides. Place the bins in the cabinet, with spacers between and on both sides. For smoother movement, sand the notches, if necessary.

APPLY FINISHING TOUCHES. Fill in all voids and countersunk screw holes with wood putty. Finish-sand the cabinet and bins with fine-grit sandpaper. For a finish, choose an enamel with a medium gloss or eggshell finish to make cleaning easy. When the finish is dry, install a metal bin pull on the front of each bin.

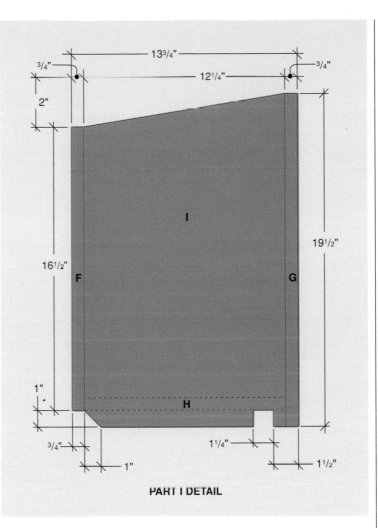

PART I DETAIL

TIP

Ensure a smooth finish by working in a well-ventilated, dust-free area. Airborne dust can ruin a painted finish. Avoid painting a project in an area where woodworking tools have recently operated, and wipe off all sanded surfaces to completely remove dust.

115

Mirrored Coat Rack

Nothing welcomes visitors to your home like an elegant,
finely crafted mirrored coat rack.

CONSTRUCTION MATERIALS

Quantity	Lumber
1	1 × 2" × 3' oak
1	1 × 3" × 4' oak
1	1 × 4" × 3' oak
1	1 × 6" × 3' oak
1	½ × ¾" × 4' egg-and-dart molding
1	¼" × 2 × 4' plywood

An entryway or foyer seems naked without a coat rack and a mirror, and this simple oak project gives you both features in one striking package. The egg-and-dart beading at the top and the decorative porcelain and brass coat hooks provide just enough design interest to make the project elegant without overwhelming the essential simplicity of the look.

We used inexpensive red oak to build our mirrored coat rack, but if you are willing to invest a little more money, use quarter-sawn white oak to create an item with the look of a true antique. For a special touch, have the edges of the mirror beveled at the glass store.

116

OVERALL SIZE:
22¾" HIGH
32" LONG
1½" DEEP

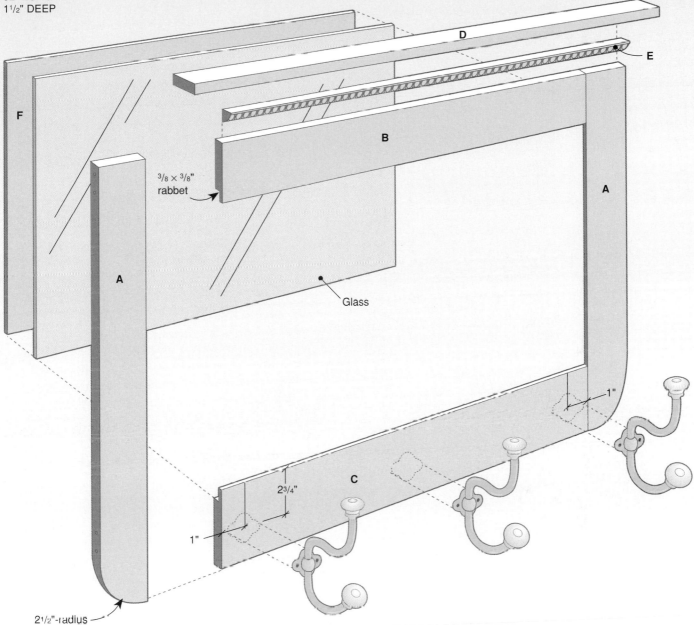

D

B

E

F

³⁄₈ × ³⁄₈"
rabbet

A

A

Glass

1"

C

2¾"

1"

2½"-radius
roundover

Cutting List

Key	Part	Dimension	Pcs.	Material
A	Stile	¾ × 2½ × 22"	2	Oak
B	Top rail	¾ × 3½ × 24"	1	Oak
C	Bottom rail	¾ × 5½ × 24"	1	Oak
D	Cap	¾ × 1½ × 32"	1	Oak
E	Molding	½ × ¾ × 29"	1	Oak
F	Mirror back	¼ × 13¾ × 24¾"	1	Plywood

Materials: ⅛ × 13¾ × 24¾" mirror, wood glue, ¼ × 36" oak
doweling, #6 × 1½" wood screws, coat hooks with screws (3),
1" wire brads.

Note: Measurements reflect the actual thickness of dimensional lumber.

Clamp the frame components together, then drill 3½"-deep guide holes for the through-dowel joints.

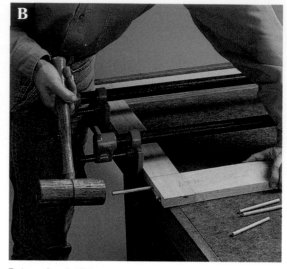

Drive glued 4"-long oak dowels into the guide holes to make the dowel joints.

Mount a belt sander to your worksurface, and use it as a grinder to smooth out the roundover cuts on the frame.

Directions: Mirrored Coat Rack

MAKE THE MIRROR FRAME. Start by cutting the frame components to size. Cut the stiles (A) to length from 1 × 3 oak. Cut the top rail (B) from 1 × 4 oak and cut the bottom rail (C) from 1 × 6 oak. Sand the stiles and rails with medium sandpaper (100- or 120-grit) to smooth out rough spots, then finish-sand with fine sandpaper (150- or 180-grit). We used through-dowel joints to hold the frame parts together.

Lay the rails between the stiles on your worksurface to form a frame. Square the frame, then use pipe or bar clamps to hold it together. Drill two ¼"-dia. × 3½"-deep holes at each joint, drilling through the stiles and into the rails **(photo A).** Now, cut eight 4"-long oak dowels. Apply glue and drive dowels into holes, using a wood mallet so you don't break the dowels **(photo B).** Once the glue has dried, re-move the clamps, trim off the ends of the dowels with a back-saw, sand them level with the wood surface and scrape off excess glue.

ROUND OVER THE FRAME ENDS. On the bottom end of each stile, lay out an arc with a 2½" radius (see *Diagram*) to mark the decorative roundovers. Cut along the arc line using a jig saw, and smooth out the cut with a belt sander mounted to your worksurface **(photo C).**

DRILL MOUNTING HOLES & CUT THE MIRROR RECESS. Before you attach the decorative top cap, drill ⅜"-diameter counter-

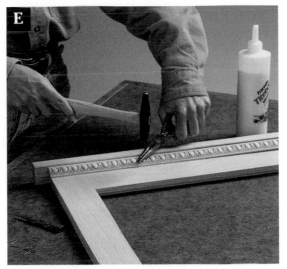

Use a router with a ⅜" piloted rabbeting bit to cut a recess for the mirror in the frame back.

Center egg-and-dart trim molding under the cap, and attach with glue and 2d finish nails.

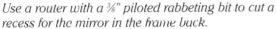

Install the mirror and mirror back, then secure them to the frame with wire brads, driven with a brad pusher.

nails driven with a tack hammer **(photo E).** Set the nail heads. Sand all sharp edges on the frame.

INSTALL THE MIRROR. Set the mirror into the recess in the frame. Cut ¼"-thick plywood to make the mirror back (F), and set it over the back of the mirror. Secure the mirror and mirror back with 1" wire brads driven into the edges of the frame **(photo F).**

TIP

Try to hit a wall stud with at least one mounting screw when hanging heavy objects on a wall. Use 3"-long screws when attaching to wall studs and use toggle bolts to mount where no studs are present.

bored screw holes through the top rail, so you can attach the mirrored coat rack to a wall. Next, cut a rabbet around the back edge of the inside frame, using a router and ⅜" piloted rabbet bit. Set the depth of the cut at ½" **(photo D).** Square off the corners of the rabbet with a wood chisel.

INSTALL THE CAP & MOLDING. Cut the cap (D) to length from 1 × 2 oak and attach it to the

top of the top rail, flush with the back edge, using glue and counterbored wood screws. Make sure the cap overhangs the stiles evenly on the ends (1½" per end).

Cut a piece of oak egg-and-dart-style trim (E), or any other trim style you prefer, to length. Sand a slight, decorative bevel at each end. Attach the molding tight against the underside of the cap, centered side to side, using glue and 2d finish

APPLY FINISHING TOUCHES. Fill all counterbores with oak plugs and sand flush with the wood surface. Apply stain and topcoat as desired. When dry, install the coat hooks (see *Diagram*). Hang the coat rack (see *Tip*, above).

Coffee Table

If you have ever built a picture frame, you already have most of the skills needed to make this clean and simple coffee table.

CONSTRUCTION MATERIALS

Quantity	Lumber
2	1 × 2" × 8' pine
1	1 × 2" × 10' pine
1	¾ × ¾" × 4' pine
2	¾" × 2 × 4' birch plywood
2	½ × 2¼" × 8' beaded pine casing

Some coffee tables are so ornate and expensive that you would never dare come near them with a hot beverage. This coffee table has a beauty all its own, but it is meant to be used—and used and used and used again. Made from birch plywood and topcoated with polyurethane, the tabletop will stand up to just about any abuse you care to inflict upon it. Even the plain pine structure, painted with white enamel, resists the effects of spilled drinks and heavy shoes.

But the best feature of this sturdy little table is that it is un-compromisingly easy to build. The table base, made from dimensional pine, requires only straight cuts and butt joints that are screwed and glued.

120

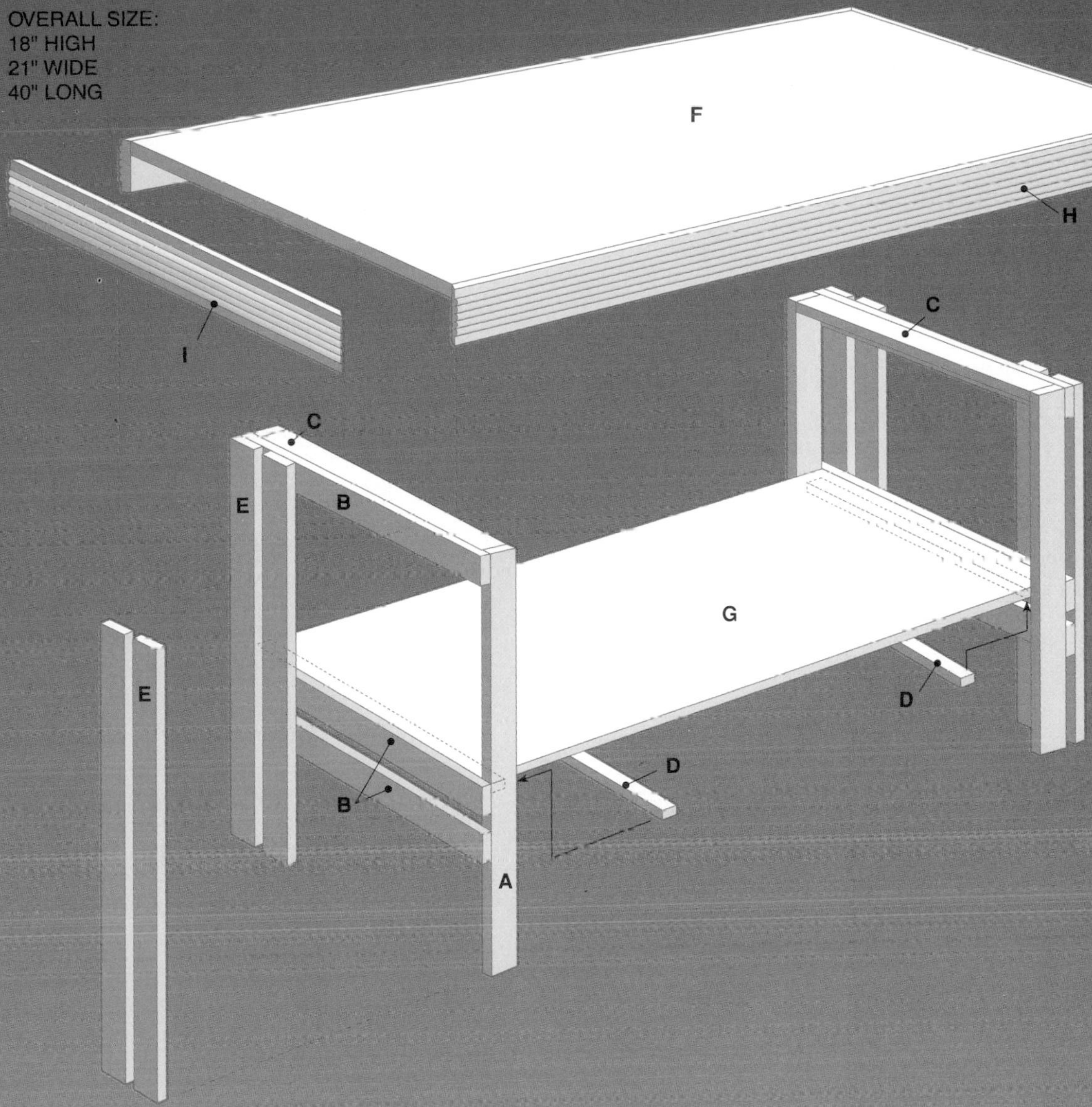

OVERALL SIZE:
18" HIGH
21" WIDE
40" LONG

F

H

I

C

E

B

E

G

D

A

B

D

A

Cutting List				
Key	Part	Dimension	Pcs.	Material
A	Post	¾ × 1½ × 17¼"	4	Pine
B	Rail	¾ × 1½ × 15"	6	Pine
C	Top cleat	¾ × 1½ × 13½"	2	Pine
D	Shelf cleat	¾ × ¾ × 13"	2	Pine
E	Slat	¾ × 1½ × 17¼"	8	Pine

Cutting List				
Key	Part	Dimension	Pcs.	Material
F	Top	¾ × 20 × 39"	1	Birch plywood
G	Shelf	¾ × 13½ × 30½"	1	Birch plywood
H	Side apron	½ × 2¼ × 40"	2	Beaded pine casing
I	End apron	½ × 2¼ × 21"	2	Beaded pine casing

Materials: Glue, #8 × 1¼" wood screws, finish nails (2d, 4d), ¾"-wide birch veneer tape, tack-on glides, finishing materials.

Note: Measurements reflect the actual size of dimensional lumber.

Mount the top rail flush with the post ends and the bottom and middle rails on the layout marks.

Fasten the slats to the rails with glue and by driving screws through the inside face of the rails into the slats.

Directions: Coffee Table

BUILD THE FRAME. Start by cutting the posts (A) to length from 1 × 2 pine. Sand the faces and edges of the posts and round over the corners with 80-grit sandpaper. Measure up from the bottom of each post 3" and 6", and place marks on the edges of the posts for the rail positions. Next, cut the rails (B) to length from 1 × 2 pine. Sand the faces and edges of the rails and round over the corners with 80-grit sandpaper. Lay two posts on edge on a flat surface. Position a rail flush with the top ends of the posts and flush with the outside edges of the posts. Fasten the rail to the posts with glue and #8 × 1¼" wood screws. Position two more rails at the previously marked locations on the posts and attach the rails to the posts with glue and wood screws **(photo A).** Drive

TIP

Use appropriately sized scrap pieces of dimensional lumber as spacers during assembly procedures to keep components properly aligned.

the screws through the rails into the posts. Use two screws at each end of each rail. When the first rail-and-post assembly is constructed, use the same steps to build the other rail-and-post assembly. Next, cut the slats (E) to length from 1 × 2 pine. Sand the faces and edges of the rails and round over the corners with 80-grit sandpaper. Lay four slats facedown on a flat surface. Place the rail and post assemblies on top of the

slats, with the rails resting on the slat faces. Position one slat even with the ends of the rails, so the top end is flush with the top edge of the top rail, and fasten with glue and screws. Drive the screws through the inside face of the rails and into the slats to conceal the screw heads. Position another slat ¾" away from the first slat, keeping the top end flush with the top rail, and secure with glue and screws **(photo B).** Now, on the

Attach the cleats by screwing through the cleat into the rail. The bottom of the cleat should be flush with the bottom edge of the rail.

opposite end of the rail-and-post assembly, position a slat flush with the outside end of the rails and flush with the top edge of the top rail. Fasten the slat in place, then position another slat ¾" away from the first slat, keeping the top flush with the top rail, and secure the slat with glue and screws. Be sure to drive the screws through the rails and into the slats in order to keep the screw heads concealed.

MAKE & ATTACH THE CLEATS. Cut the top cleats (C) to length from 1 × 2 pine lumber and the shelf cleats (D) to length from ¾ × ¾" pine molding. On the insides of the rail-and-post assemblies, mark a line ¾" down from the top edge of the middle rail. This will allow the shelf to sit on the cleats and be flush with the top of the middle rails. Position the cleats on the layout lines, and fasten with glue and screws **(photo C)**. The bottoms of the cleats should be flush with the bottoms of the middle rails. Then attach the top cleats to the top rail and the posts.

MAKE THE TOP. Start by cutting the top (F) from birch plywood, using a circular saw and straightedge **(photo D)**. When cutting plywood sheets, it is helpful to set the plywood on scrap lumber, usually 2 × 4s, to give the saw blade clearance between the plywood and the top of the worksurface. With this technique, you can clamp the plywood to the worksurface and have a stable surface for cutting without fear of the cutout piece falling on the floor and getting damaged. Use a power sander to smooth the edges of the top so the apron pieces will have a flat, square edge to be attached to.

MAKE & ATTACH THE APRONS TO THE TOP. Start by cutting a 45° miter on one end of the apron molding material with a power miter box **(photo E)** or with a miter box and backsaw. Cut the miter so the angle goes away from the inside surface of the molding. Lay the top on a flat surface with the top facedown. Position the apron molding against a long edge of the top, holding the heel of the miter tight to the corner of the top. With the

TIP

A straightedge is a useful tool for making accurate, straight cuts. Store-bought straightedges are highly accurate and very durable, since they are usually fashioned from metal. But for many cutting jobs, a long, straight piece of scrap lumber (2 × 4s are a good choice) clamped to your workpiece makes a perfectly serviceable straightedge.

molding held tightly in place, mark the other corner position along the edge and onto the back side of the apron molding. Cut a 45° miter at this

Use scrap pieces of 2 x 4 lumber to elevate the plywood off of the worksurface top and to keep from cutting into the top with the saw.

Use a power miter box to cut 45° miters on the ends of the apron molding. Keep the molding tight to the fence to ensure clean cuts.

Measure the inset for the frame assemblies, then secure to the top with glue and screws driven through the top rail into the tabletop.

mark, so the heel of the miter lines up with the mark and the toe (the pointy part) of the miter goes away from the mark. Using glue and 4d finish nails, fasten the side apron (H) that you just cut to length to the edge of the top, keeping the top surface flush with the top edge of the apron. Now, cut another 45° miter on the end of the apron molding. Place the

molding against the edge of the short end of the top, tight to the miter on the attached side apron. Mark the location of the edge corner on the back side of the apron molding and cut a 45° miter at the mark. Fasten the end apron (I) that you just cut to length to the edge of the top, using glue and 4d finish nails. Keep the top edge of the apron flush with the top surface of the top. Cut another 45° miter on the end of the apron molding. Place the molding against the edge of the long side of the top, tight to the miter on the attached end apron. Mark the location of the edge corner on the back side of the apron molding and cut a 45° miter at the back side of the apron molding, at the mark. Fasten the side apron to the edge of the top using glue and

4d finish nails. Keep the top edge of the apron flush with the top surface of the top. Cut a 45° miter on the end of the apron molding. Place the molding on the bottom edges of the side aprons, with one end fitted into the miter and the other resting on the edge of the side apron so it lines up with the edge of the top and the miter. It can be a little tricky getting a piece that is mitered at both ends to fit perfectly between two mitered pieces. You'll be better off to mark and cut the last end apron a little long, then test-fit it in the frame and trim it down a little if needed. When it fits properly, fasten the end apron to the edge of the top with glue and nails. At each mitered corner, lock-nail the apron miters with 2d finish nails to keep them from separating due to humidity changes (see *Tip*, left).

ATTACH THE TOP TO THE FRAME. Start by cutting the shelf (G) to size from birch plywood, using a circular saw and straightedge. With the tabletop upside down on the worksurface, position the frame assemblies upside down on the bottom side of the top. Place the shelf, on the top cleats, between the frame assemblies to provide proper spacing for the layout. Measure and mark the inset for the frame assembly on the bottom side of the top. Measure in from the inside of the end aprons 2¾", and 2½" in from the inside of the side aprons, and place marks **(photo F)**. Position the frame assemblies on the marks. Fasten the frame assemblies to the top using #6 × 1¼" screws through the top cleats into the tabletop.

APPLY VENEER TAPE TO THE SHELF. Smooth all four edges of the shelf using a power sander. The edges need to be smooth and square for the veneer tape to adhere properly. Clamp the shelf on edge on your worksurface. Cut strips of ¾" birch veneer tape to fit the shelf edges, then set them in place and iron them onto the edges with a household iron **(photo G).** The heat from the iron activates the adhesive backing, and the downward pressure helps create a firm bond. Follow the iron with a flat wooden block to smooth and set the tape. When the adhesive has cooled, trim the veneer tape, if needed, so it is flush with the surfaces of the plywood. Then, sand the edges and corners with medium (100- or 120-grit) sandpaper. Be careful not to oversand or you may wear through the veneer tape.

INSTALL THE SHELF. Turn the tabletop and frame assemblies right-side up and apply glue to the top edge of the cleats and the inside of the middle rail. Position the shelf into place on the cleats between the posts and rails. Secure the shelf in position by driving 4d finish nails through the posts and middle rails, and into the shelf edges **(photo H).** Countersink the nail heads with a nail set and hammer. Be careful when pounding in the nails so you don't mar the posts and rails.

APPLY THE FINISHING TOUCHES. When the coffee table is completely assembled, fill all exposed nail holes with a quality wood filler. Sand the dried putty level with the wood surface, then sand out any rough spots, especially on the table-

Apply self-adhesive veneer tape to the shelf edges, using a household iron to heat up the tape and press it in position.

Fasten the coffee table shelf to the frame assemblies with glue and 4d finish nails.

top, with medium (100- or 120-grit) sandpaper. Finish-sand the entire coffee table with fine (150- or 180-grit) sandpaper. Finish the coffee table as desired. We chose a combination of finishes for our coffee table. First, we applied three light coats of semi-gloss polyurethane to the tabletop, leaving the natural color of the birch essentially unchanged. Then, we painted the rest of the coffee table with enamel paint

to create contrast with the tabletop. After finishing, fasten tack-on glides to the bottoms of the posts.

Mission Lamp Base

The beauty and texture of oak combines with a simple style and charm in this traditional table lamp.

PROJECT
POWER TOOLS

This decorative lamp base provides just the right accent for a family room tabletop or bedside stand. It's made of red oak, and the design is simple and stylish. The clean vertical lines of the oak slats are rooted in the popular Mission style. Clearly, our lamp base will be an enjoyable project that you and your entire family can enjoy for a long time. The oak parts are joined with glue and nails, so the lamp base goes together with a minimum of time and fuss.

Once the base is assembled, just insert the lamp hardware, which you can buy at any local hardware store, and you're ready to turn it on. Lamp hardware kits include all the components you need to make your project functional—harp, socket, cord and tubing. Make sure you follow manufacturer's directions when installing the hardware. When you're finished, buy an attractive shade, either contemporary or classic, and set the lamp on a nightstand or table.

CONSTRUCTION MATERIALS

Quantity	Lumber
1	1 × 8" × 2' oak
2	1 × 2" × 10' oak
1	1 × 3 × 12" oak

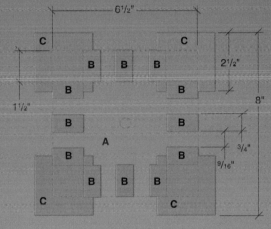

6½"

2½"

1½"

8"

¾"

9/16"

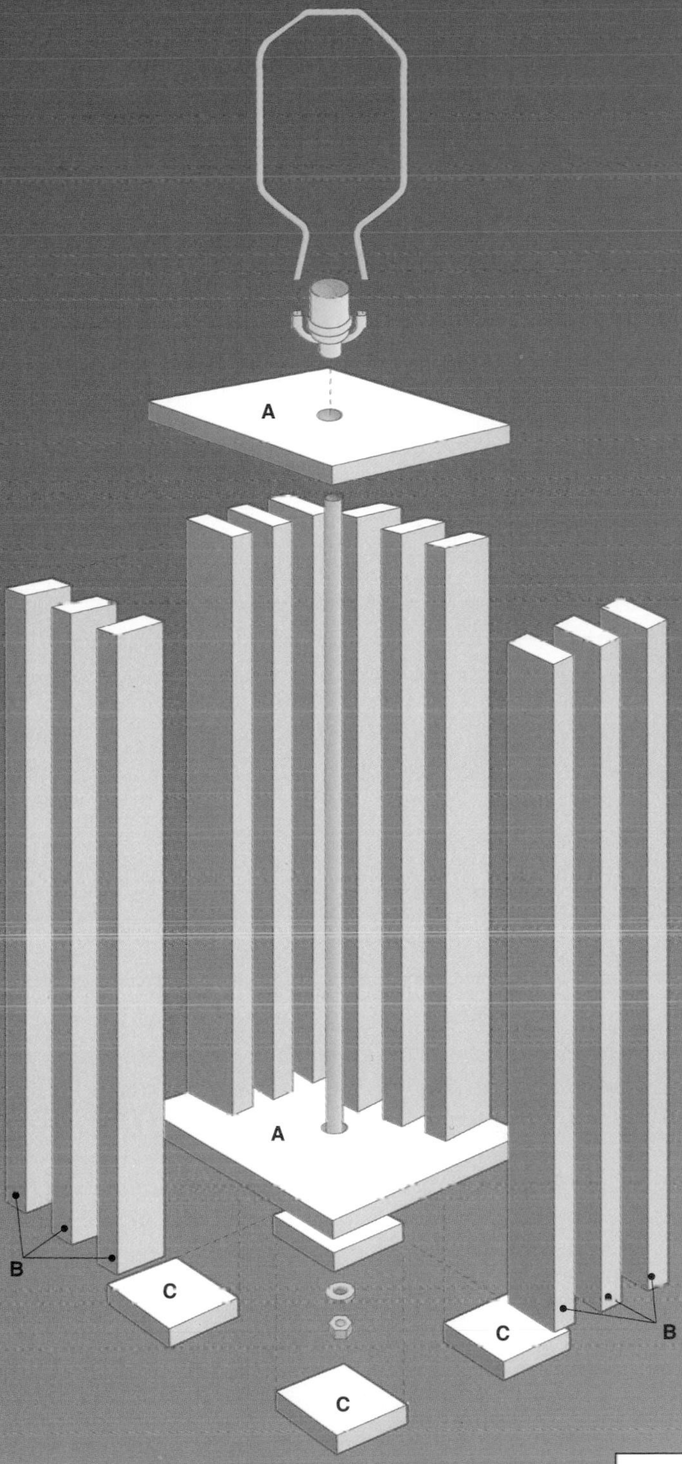

PLAN VIEW

Cutting List				
Key	**Part**	**Dimension**	**Pcs.**	**Material**
A	Plate	¾ × 6½ × 6½"	2	Oak
B	Slat	¾ × 1½ × 17"	12	Oak
C	Foot	¾ × 2½ × 2½"	4	Oak

Materials: Wood glue, 6d finish nails, lamp hardware kit, finishing materials.

Note: Measurements reflect the actual size of dimensional lumber.

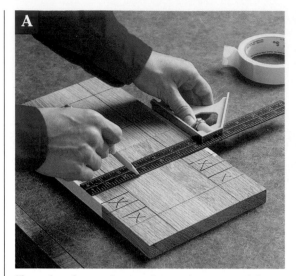

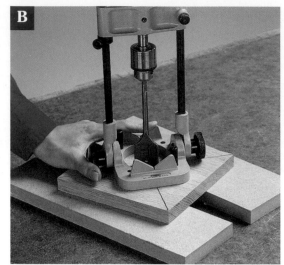

Tape the plates edge-to-edge and use a straight-edge to lay out and mark the slat positions.

Use a portable drill guide to make accurate center holes in the plates.

Drill pilot holes through the plates in position for 6d finish nails.

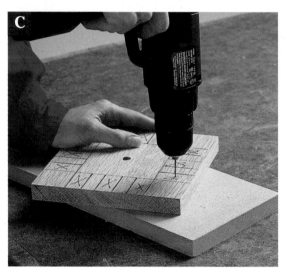

Directions: Lamp Base

PREPARE THE PLATES & SLATS. There aren't many parts in the lamp base, but you need to measure and mark accurately before assembling them. You must locate the exact centers of the bases, and position the slats so they are evenly spaced between them. Start by cutting

the plates (A) and slats (B) to size. Sand out rough edges with medium-grit (over 120) sandpaper, then finish-sand with fine-grit (150 or 180) sandpaper. Since only one side of each slat will be fully visible on the assembled project, make sure they have at least one clean, or knot-free, edge. Lay the plates edge-to-edge with their sides aligned, and tape or clamp them in place (see *Diagram*, page 127). Lay out the slat placement on the plates **(photo A).** Use a straightedge and pencil to draw lines diagonally from corner to corner on

both plates to locate their centers. Drill a 1-dia. × ¼"-deep counterbore hole on the bottom center of the lower plate **(photo B),** using a spade bit. This hole is made to make room for a washer when you assemble the lamp. Drill a ⅜"-dia. hole through the center of the ¼"-deep hole, and through the center of the other plate for the lamp tube. Use a drill with a ¹⁄₁₆"-dia. bit to make pilot holes for finish nails through the plates to secure the slats **(photo C).** Each slat should have two finish nails attaching it to the plates. To make sure all the holes in the plates are completely straight, use a portable drill guide, which keeps the drill stationary at the desired drilling angle.

ATTACH THE PLATES & SLATS. Attaching the plates and slats can be done quickly and easily with a few drops of glue and some 6d finish nails. Once all the slats have been attached to the plates, you need only attach the feet (C) to complete the lamp frame. Apply glue to the top edge of each slat and attach them, one at a time, to the top plate. Fasten the slats to the plate by driving finish nails through the holes you drilled when preparing the parts **(photo D).** Use a nail set to set the finish nails deeper into the holes, and fill the holes with oak-tinted wood putty. For best results, fasten each slat with one nail, then check the positioning. Make any needed adjustments, and secure each slat with a second finish nail. Fasten the lower plate, with the 1"-dia. × ¼"-deep counterbore hole on the bottom, and repeat the nailing procedure. Set and fill the nail holes.

ATTACH THE FEET. Begin by cutting the feet (C) to size and sanding them to finished smoothness. For economy, we cut them from the same 1 × 8 board we used to make the plates. Measure and mark a line ¾" from the outside edge on two adjacent sides of each foot. These lines show where each plate corner is positioned on the feet (for more information on the feet placement, see *Diagram*, page 127). Like the slats, the feet are attached with finish nails and glue. Drill two holes for finish nails through each foot. Attach the feet to the plate with glue and nails, making sure the feet are properly aligned. Set and fill the nail holes, and sand the surfaces to finished smoothness.

INSTALL THE HARDWARE. Now that the lamp base is completely assembled, you need to insert the hardware that will make the project fully functional. You can buy a lamp socket kit at most hardware stores. The kit usually includes a harp for attaching a shade, a socket, lamp cord and a ⅜"-dia.

Attach the slats to the top plate with glue and 6d finish nails.

Attach the threaded lamp tube with a washer and nut to secure the tube to the lamp frame.

threaded lamp tube. Begin by cutting the lamp tube to length so that it extends from plate to plate. Insert the tube through the holes in the plates. Attach the harp to the top plate, and secure the tube to the bottom plate with a washer and nut **(photo E).** Thread the cord through the tube, and attach it according to manufacturer's directions.

APPLY THE FINISHING TOUCHES. The lamp is a decorative item, so you'll want to put a nice finish on the completed project. Finish the lamp as desired. We used light oak stain, then added two coats of wipe-on tung oil topcoat. Finally, apply felt pads to the bottom of the feet to prevent scratching on tabletop surfaces.

Corner Display Stand

This light and airy unit brings hardworking display shelving to any cramped corner of your house.

The open back on this corner display stand lets you add a lot of display space to any room, without adding a lot of weight to the decor. Its roomy shelves are perfect for flower vases, fine china, souvenir-ware, picture frames and other knickknacks and collectibles.

CONSTRUCTION MATERIALS

Quantity	Lumber
7	1 × 4" × 8' pine
1	¾" × 4' × 8' plywood
1	¾ × ¾" × 6' cove molding

But this corner display stand is much more than a practical space-saver. The gentle arches on the front and the slatted back design blend into just about any decorating style. And because it's such a simple design, it doesn't draw attention away from the items on display.

This corner display stand is also very inexpensive to build. A single sheet of plywood is more than enough to make the triangular shelves, and the shelf rails and standards are made from 1 × 4 pine. The decorative trim pieces on the edges of the shelves are cut from ordinary ¾" cove molding. These materials, together with the painted finish, give the display stand a contemporary style. But if you're looking for furnishings with a more formal appearance, substitute oak boards and oak plywood, then apply a warm-toned wood stain.

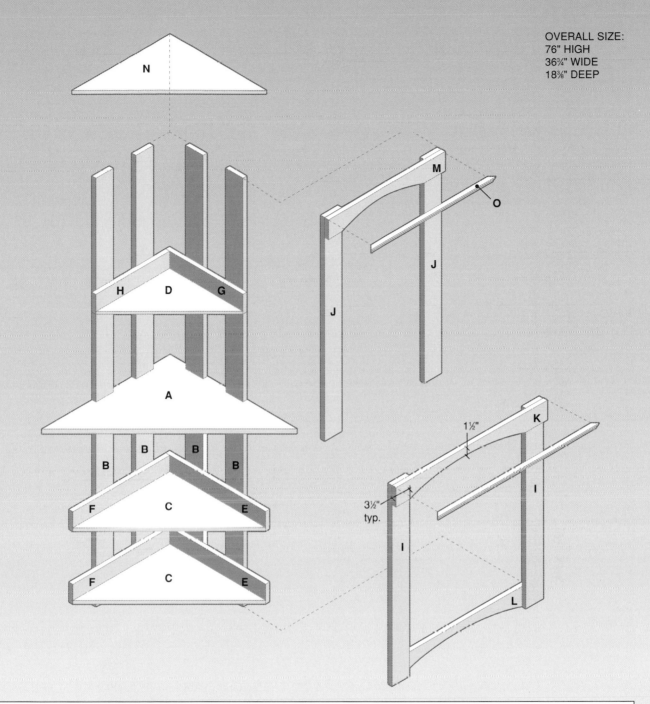

OVERALL SIZE:
76" HIGH
36¾" WIDE
18⅜" DEEP

Key	Part	Dimension	Pcs.	Material
A	Center shelf	¾ × 26 × 26"	1	Plywood
B	Standard	¾ × 3½ × 75¼"	4	Pine
C	Bottom shelf	¾ × 19½ × 19½"	2	Plywood
D	Top shelf	¾ × 15 × 15"	1	Plywood
E	Bottom rail	¾ × 3½ × 20¼"	2	Pine
F	Bottom rail	¾ × 3½ × 19½"	2	Pine
G	Top rail	¾ × 3½ × 15¾"	1	Pine
H	Top rail	¾ × 3½ × 15"	1	Pine

Key	Part	Dimension	Pcs.	Material
I	Lower stile	¾ × 3½ × 35¼"	2	Pine
J	Upper stile	¾ × 3½ × 39¼"	2	Pine
K	Lower front rail	¾ × 3½ × 32"	1	Pine
L	Lower front rail	¾ × 3½ × 30¼"	1	Pine
M	Upper front rail	¾ × 3½ × 25¼"	1	Pine
N	Top	¾ × 21¼ × 21¼"	1	Plywood
O	Trim	¾ × ¾ × 35"*	2	Cove molding

Materials: Wood glue, wood screws (#6 × 1½", #6 × 2"), 1¼" brads, finishing materials.
Note: Measurements reflect the actual size of dimensional lumber.   *Cut to fit.

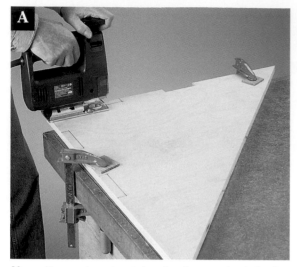

Use a jig saw to cut notches for the standards in the back edges of the center shelf.

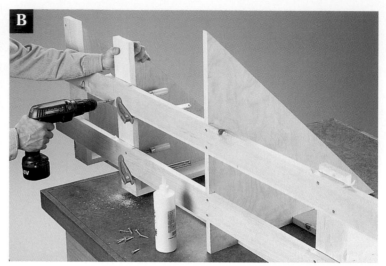

Drive screws through the standards and into the shelf rails.

Directions: Corner Display Stand

MAKE THE SHELVES. To make the center shelf (A), use a circular saw with a straightedge guide to cut a 26⅛" plywood square in half diagonally. The result is two triangles with 26"-long sides (the extra ⅛" allows for the thickness of the saw blade). Use a square to lay out ¾ × 3½"-long notches for the standards on the shelf sides, starting 4" and 12¼" in from each 90° corner, on each side. Cut the notches with a jig saw **(photo A).** Sand the shelf to remove any rough spots. To make the bottom shelves, cut a 19⅝"-square plywood piece in half diagonally. Cut the top shelf (D) to form a right triangle with two 15" sides. The top and bottom shelves are fitted with rails along the back edges. Cut the bottom rails (E, F) and the top rails (G, H) to length from 1 × 4 pine. Attach one longer rail (E) and one shorter rail (F) to the back edges of each bottom shelf so they make a butt joint and are flush with the ends of the shelf. Use glue and #6 × 2"

Use a flexible marking guide to draw the arches in the front rails.

Assemble the arched front rails and the stiles into face frames.

wood screws. Countersink all the screw pilot holes. Attach a longer top rail (G) and shorter top rail (H) to the back edges of the top shelf, so the bottoms are flush.

ATTACH THE STANDARDS. Cut the standards (B) to length. Sand the legs, and clamp them together with their tops and bottoms flush. Draw reference lines across the standards 3½",

16", 35¼" and 52" from one end. Then, draw reference lines on the shelf rails, 3¼" and 11½" on each side of the corner to mark the positions of the inside edges of the standards. Clamp the shelves to the standards so the reference lines are aligned, then attach the standards to the shelves with glue and #6 × 2" wood screws, driven through pilot holes in the backs of the standards and into the shelves **(photo B).** Note that the center shelf should be installed so the notches fit over the standards.

BUILD THE FACE FRAMES. The face frames give a finished look to the front of the display stand. They consist of vertical boards, called stiles, and horizontal boards, called rails. The rails feature decorative arcs. Cut the lower stiles (I), upper stiles (J), lower front rails (K, L) and upper front rail (M) to length. An easy way to mark the top and bottom arches is to use a thin, flexible piece of metal, plastic or wood as a marking guide. Find the centerpoint of each rail, and mark a point 13" in from the center in both directions. Tack a 1¼" brad at these points, as close to a long edge as possible. Also tack a brad at the centerpoint of each workpiece, 2" up from the same long edge. Hook the marking guide over the middle brad, and flex each end of the guide to the marked points. Trace the curve on each rail **(photo C),** and cut the curves with a jig saw. Position the shorter of the two lower front rails (L) across the lower stiles, with the arc pointing down. The edge of the rail containing the arc should be flush with the ends of the stiles, and the rail should be ⅞"

in from the outside edges of each stile (see *Diagram,* page 131). This is the bottom of the face frame. Clamp the rail to the stiles. Then, clamp the longer of the lower front rails (K) to the tops of the stiles, with the straight edge flush with the tops. The ends of the rail should be flush with the edges of the stile. Attach the lower front rails to the lower stiles with four #6 × 1¼" screws driven at each joint **(photo D).** Attach the upper front rail to the tops of the upper stiles, so the top and side edges are flush.

ATTACH THE FACE FRAMES & TOP. With the stand upright, slip the lower face frame in position. The bottom rail should fit beneath the lowest shelf, and the top rail should fit beneath the center shelf. Center the face frame from side to side so the overhang is equal. Clamp the face frame to the stand, then attach it with #6 × 2" wood screws driven through the stiles and into the edges of the shelves, and also driven into the top of each rail through the shelf above it **(photo E).** Position the upper face frame so

the bottoms of the stiles rest on the center shelf, and the stiles overhang the ends of the top shelf by equal amounts. Tack the face frame in place by driving one #6 × 2" wood screw through each stile and into the front edge of the top shelf. Then, drive screws up through the underside of the center shelf and into the bottom ends of the stiles **(photo F).**

APPLY FINISHING TOUCHES. Cut the top (N) to size, and attach it to the tops of the standards and the top rail of the upper face frame with glue and screws. The back sides of the top should be flush with the outside faces of the standards. To make the trim pieces (O), cut strips of ¾" cove molding to fit along the front edges of the center shelf and top shelf, with the ends miter-cut to follow the line of each shelf. Attach the trim pieces with 1¼" brads driven into pilot holes. Set all nail heads, then cover the nail and screw heads with wood putty. Sand the corner display stand, and paint with primer and two coats of enamel paint.

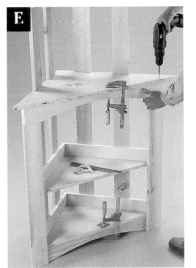

Drive screws through the center shelf and into the face frame.

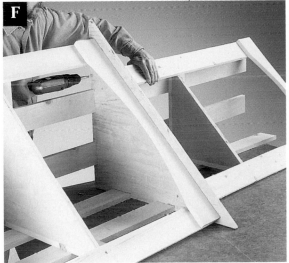

Drive wood screws up through the center shelf to secure the upper stiles.

133

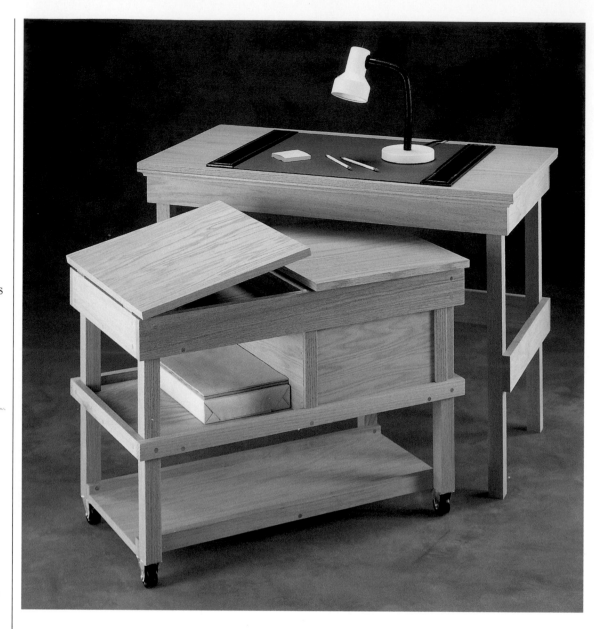

Nesting Office

The basic building blocks of a home office, designed to fit together in one small space.

CONSTRUCTION MATERIALS

Quantity	Lumber
3	2 × 2" × 8' oak
4	1 × 4" × 8' oak
2	1 × 2" × 8' oak
4	¾" × 2 × 4' oak plywood
1	⅜ × 1¹⁄₁₆" × 6' oak stop molding
2	¾ × ¾" × 8' oak cove molding

The desk and credenza are the two principal furnishings needed in any home office. This nesting office pair features both components at full size, but because they fit together they can be stored in about the same amount of space as a standard medium-size desk. Made of oak and oak plywood, both pieces are well

constructed and pleasing to the eye. The desk has a large writing surface, and the credenza is a versatile rolling storage cabinet with a hanging-file box, and shelves for storage of books, paper and other material. A flip-up top lets you use the credenza as an auxiliary writing or computer surface, and still store office supplies below.

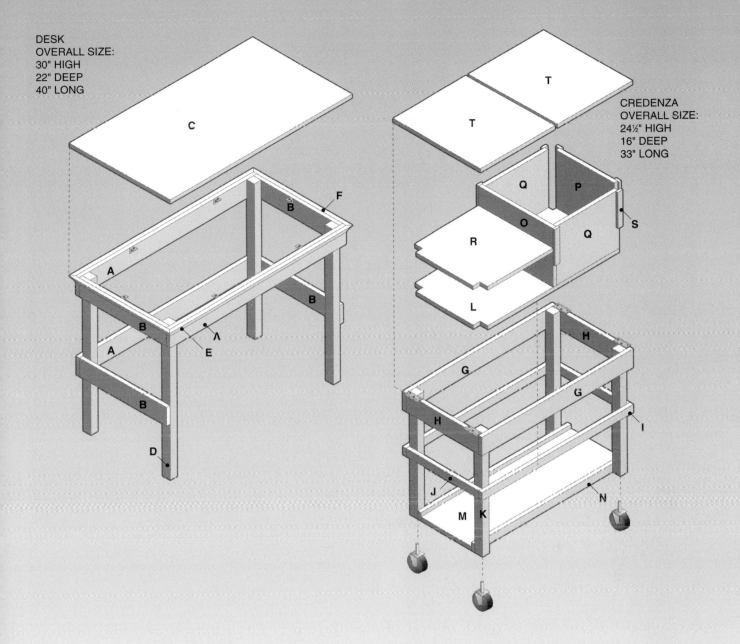

DESK
OVERALL SIZE:
30" HIGH
22" DEEP
40" LONG

CREDENZA
OVERALL SIZE:
24½" HIGH
16" DEEP
33" LONG

Key	Part	Dimension	Pcs.	Material
A	Desk side	¾ × 3½ × 38"	3	Oak
B	Desk end	¾ × 3½ × 19"	4	Oak
C	Desktop	¾ × 22 × 40"	1	Plywood
D	Desk leg	1½ × 1½ × 29¼"	4	Oak
E	Side molding	¾ × ¾ × 40"	2	Cove molding
F	End molding	¾ × ¾ × 22"	2	Cove molding
G	Credenza side	¾ × 3½ × 33"	2	Oak
H	Credenza end	¾ × 3½ × 16"	2	Oak
I	Middle rail	¾ × 1½ × 33"	2	Oak
J	End rail	¾ × 1½ × 16"	2	Oak

Key	Part	Dimension	Pcs.	Material
K	Credenza leg	1½ × 1½ × 21¼"	4	Oak
L	Middle shelf	¾ × 16 × 31½"	1	Plywood
M	Bottom shelf	¾ × 11½ × 31½"	1	Plywood
N	Bottom rail	¾ × 1½ × 31½"	2	Oak
O	Divider	¾ × 11¼ × 16"	1	Plywood
P	End panel	¾ × 11¼ × 13"	1	Plywood
Q	Side panel	¾ × 11¼ × 13⅞"	2	Plywood
R	Bin bottom	¾ × 15¼ × 16"	1	Plywood
S	Stop	⅜ × 1¹⁄₁₆ × 7"	6	Stop molding
T	Bin lid	¾ × 16⅜ × 19¼"	2	Plywood

Cutting List (left) **Cutting List** (right)

Materials: Wood glue, #6 brass wood screws (¾", 1¼", 2"), 1¼" brass brads, 3 × 1½" brass hinges (4), 2½" swivel casters (4), ¾" oak edge tape (50'), 1¼" brass corner braces (6), brass lid supports (4), finishing materials.

Note: Measurements reflect the actual size of dimensional lumber.

135

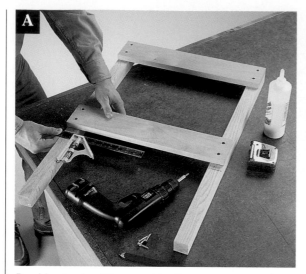

Double-check with a combination square to make sure the desk legs are square to the ends.

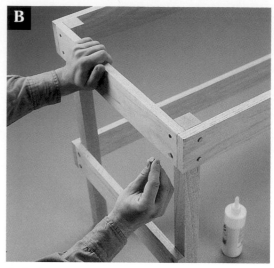

Oak plugs are glued into the counterbore recesses to cover the screw heads.

Directions:
Nesting Office

MAKE THE DESK-LEG PAIRS. The legs for the desk base are made by joining desk legs (D) to ¾"-thick boards to form two leg pairs that will be fastened together with desk side boards to compete the base. The desk ends and desk sides form a frame, called the apron, that is used to support and fasten the desktop. Start by cutting the desk ends (B) and desk legs (D) to size. Sand all parts after cutting to remove any saw marks or splinters. Lay the legs on a flat surface, arranged in pairs, then lay the desk ends across the legs to form the leg pair assemblies. One desk end in each leg pair should be flush with the tops of the legs, and

Fasten the desktop to the desk base with brass corner braces.

the bottom of the other end board should be 10½" up from the bottoms of the legs. Clamp the leg pair assemblies together, then drill two pilot holes for #6 wood screws at each joint. Center the pilot holes over the joints, keeping them at least 1" away from the tops and bottoms of the end boards. Use a counterboring bit to counterbore these and all pilot holes in the project to accept ⅜"-dia. oak wood plugs. Unclamp the parts and apply wood glue to the mating surfaces, then fasten them to-

gether with #6 × 2" brass wood screws driven through the pilot holes. Double-check the assemblies with a square to make sure the legs are square to the end boards **(photo A).**

ASSEMBLE THE DESK BASE. Cut the desk sides (A) to length and sand smooth. Drill a pair of counterbored pilot holes about 1½" in from each end of each desk side board. Before drilling the pilot holes, check the leg pairs to make sure that the screws that are driven through the pilot holes will not run into the screws that hold the end

Install strips of oak cove molding between the underside of the desktop and the desk apron. Miter the corners for a neater look.

TIP

Plain file boxes can be converted easily to hanging file boxes by installing a self-standing metal hanger system. Sold at office supply stores, the thin metal standards and support rods are custom-cut to fit the box, then assembled and set in place. The metal tabs on the hanging folders fit over the metal support rods.

boards to the legs. Adjust the pilot hole locations as needed. Apply glue to the mating end of one side board, and clamp it in place so it spans between the leg pairs, flush with the tops of the legs and desk ends. Check to make sure the leg pairs are square to the desk side, then drive #6 × 2" brass wood screws through the pilot holes. Install the other top side board the same way. Then, attach the lower side boards so the tops are flush with the tops of the end boards in the leg pairs. After the glue has set, apply glue to the ends of ⅜"-dia. oak wood plugs and insert them into all screw hole counterbores **(photo B).** When the glue has dried, sand the plugs so they are even with the surrounding wood, then sand the entire desk base with medium sandpaper to smooth out the surfaces and dull any sharp edges.

ATTACH THE DESKTOP. The plywood desktop is positioned on top of the base and fastened with corner braces. Using corner braces (without wood

glue) allows the desktop to move just enough so it will not cause the wood to split as it expands and contracts—plywood and solid oak will expand and contract at slightly different rates. Start by cutting the desktop (C) to size. Then, sand the edges so they are smooth and even. Wipe the edges clean, then cut strips of self-adhesive oak veneer edge tape to fit the edges. Use a household iron set at low to medium heat to press

the veneer onto the edges, creating edge surfaces that can accept wood stain. After the adhesive cools, trim off any excess edge tape with a sharp utility knife, then sand the veneer joints smooth with fine sandpaper. Place the desktop face down on your worksurface, and center the desk base on the desktop. The desktop should overhang the base by ¾" on all sides. Clamp the base in place, and arrange 1¼" brass corner braces along the inside edges of the desk side and end boards. Use at least two braces on the sides and one at each end. Drill pilot holes at the guide holes in the braces, then drive #6 × ¾" brass wood

Attach the credenza ends and end rails to the legs with glue and counterbored wood screws.

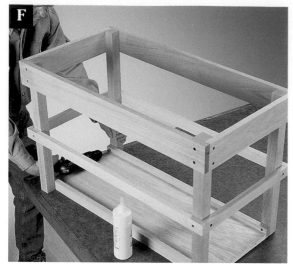

Fasten the bottom shelf by driving wood screws through the bottom rails and into the legs.

Cut notches at each corner of the middle shelf so it will fit around the credenza legs.

screws to attach the desktop **(photo C).**

ATTACH THE TOP MOLDING. The side molding (E) and end molding (F) fit underneath the desktop and are joined to the apron formed by the desk sides and ends. Cut the molding pieces to fit the desk dimensions. Miter-cut the ends of the side molding and end molding at a 45° angle. Position the side and end molding against the bottom of the desktop, and drill pilot holes in the molding for 1¼" brass brads. Apply glue to the backs of the side and end molding, including the mating surfaces of the mitered corners, and attach the molding pieces with wire brads **(photo D).**

MAKE THE CREDENZA BASE. The credenza base is built in much the same manner as the desk base. Leg pairs are formed, then joined by longer boards with wood screws and glue. Cut the credenza sides (G), credenza ends (H), middle rails (I), end rails (J) and credenza legs (K) to size. Arrange the legs in pairs with the end rails and credenza ends positioned across them.

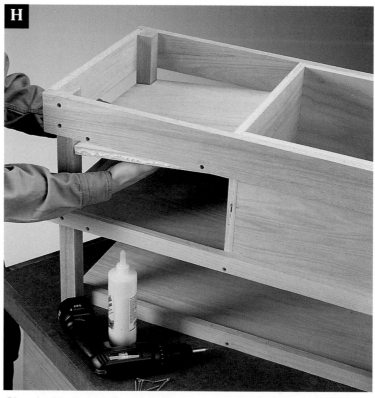

Glue the bin bottom between the credenza sides, flush with their bottom edges. Drive screws into the edges of the bin bottom to secure it.

The credenza ends should be flush with the outside edges and tops of the legs, and the end rails should be flush with the outside edges of the legs, with the tops of the rails 12" down from the tops of the legs. Clamp the parts together and drill counterbored pilot holes for #6 screws at the joints. Disassemble, apply glue to the joints, then reassemble the leg pairs and drive #6 × 2" brass wood screws through the pilot holes **(photo E).** Stand the leg pairs on edge, and position the credenza sides and middle rails across them. Attach the side

Attach strips of oak stop molding to cover the exposed plywood edges of the bins on the outside of the credenza.

rails and middle rails to the leg pairs, the same way you attached the comparable parts when building the desk base.

MAKE THE CREDENZA SHELVES. Start by cutting the middle shelf (L), bottom shelf (M) and bottom rails (N) to size. Position a bottom rail against each long side of the bottom shelf. Make sure the ends are flush, and attach the bottom rails to the bottom shelf with glue and #6 × 2" brass wood screws, driven through the bottom rails and into the bottom shelf edges. Position the bottom shelf between the credenza legs so the bottoms are flush. Drive counterbored wood screws through the bottom rails and into the credenza legs **(photo F).** Use a jig saw to cut 1½ × 1½" notches in each corner of the middle shelf, so it will fit around the credenza legs **(photo G).** To attach the middle shelf between the middle rails and end rails, apply glue to the inside edges of the middle rails and end rails, and slide the shelf into position. The middle shelf should be flush with the bottom edges of the middle rails and end

rails. Use glue and screws driven through the middle and end rails to secure the middle shelf.

MAKE THE CREDENZA BINS. The credenza bins include a file box for hanging file folders, and a supply storage box. Both bins have flip-up lids. Begin by cutting the divider (O), end panel (P), side panels (Q) and bin bottom (R) to size. Cut 1½ × 1½" notches in both corners at one end of the bin bottom so it will fit around the legs. Position the side panels and end panels in place, and secure them by driving #6 × 1¼" wood screws through the side panels and end panels and into the rails and sides. Slide the divider into place so it butts against the side panels, forming a storage box in the upper section of the credenza. Fasten the divider with wood screws. On the opposite end of the credenza, drill evenly spaced pilot holes for the bin bottom in the credenza side and end, ⅜" up from the bottom edges of the boards. Apply glue to the edges of the bin bottom and position it in place, flush with the bottom edges of the credenza sides

and ends **(photo H).** Drive #6 × 2" wood screws through the sides and ends to secure the bin bottom. Cut the stops (S) to size from oak stop molding. Drill pilot holes, and use 1¼"-long brass brads to attach the stops to the centers of the joints between the panels, legs and divider **(photo I).** Cut the lids (T) to size from a single plywood panel. Use a household iron to apply oak veneer edge tape to the edges. Do not attach the lids until after the finish has been applied.

APPLY FINISHING TOUCHES. Insert oak wood plugs into any open counterbore holes in either the desk or the credenza, and sand smooth. Give both furnishings a final finish-sanding with 180- or 220-grit sandpaper, then apply your finish of choice (you may find it easier to finish the desk if you remove the desktop first—it is important that you finish the underside as well as the top). We used a clear topcoat only for a light, contemporary look, but you may prefer to use a light or medium wood stain first. When the finish has dried, reinstall the desktop. Fasten 3 × 1½" brass hinges to the bottom faces of the credenza lids, 2¼" in from the side edges. The backs of the hinge barrels should be flush with the back edges of the lids, when closed. Attach the lids to the credenza by fastening the hinges to the credenza ends. Attach sliding lid supports to the lids and credenza sides to hold the lids open while you reach in the bins. Finally, attach a 2½" swivel caster (brass housings will look best) to the bottom of each credenza leg.

Blanket Chest

*This traditional blanket chest is also just the right
size to serve as a coffee table.*

CONSTRUCTION MATERIALS

Quantity	Lumber
1	¾" × 4 × 8' plywood
1	½ × 1⅜" × 7' stop molding
1	¼ × 1⁵⁄₁₆" × 7' corner molding
2	¾ × 1⅜" × 7' shelf cap

This roomy blanket chest
makes the most of valu-
able floor space in your
den or family room. Large
enough to hold several blankets, sheets and afghans, this
chest also makes a fine coffee
table when closed.

The blanket chest is a very
simple project, made from four
plywood panels, top and bottom panels and some decorative trim molding. For a nice,
contemporary appearance, we
chose to paint our blanket
chest in soft pastel tones. If you
paint your blanket chest as
well, be sure to use glossy
enamel paint—enamel paint
finishes are easiest to clean.
Another finishing option for
the blanket chest is to line the
interior with aromatic cedar
liners to discourage moths and
give blankets and other textiles
a fresh scent. Aromatic cedar
liners are sold in 4 × 8 sheets
and self-adhesive strips.

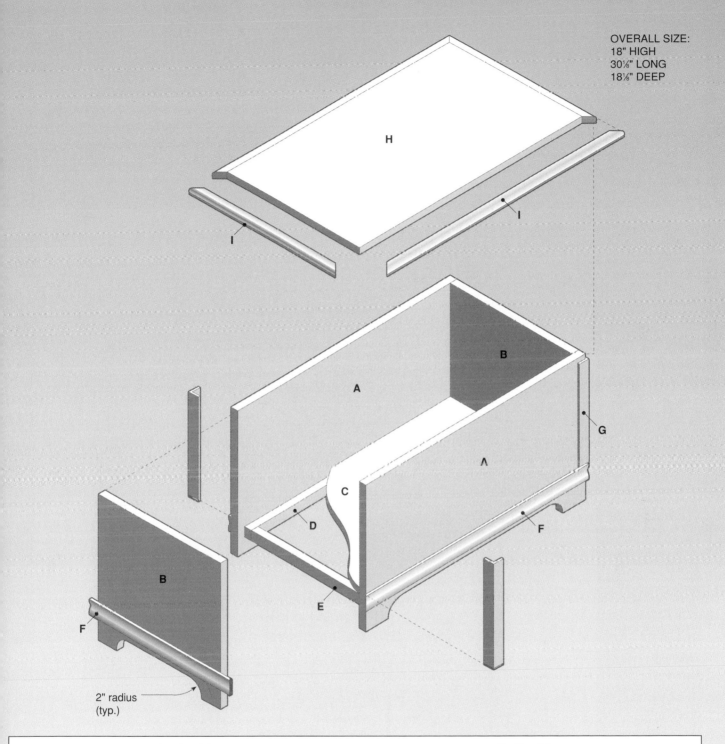

OVERALL SIZE:
18" HIGH
30⅛" LONG
18⅛" DEEP

2" radius
(typ.)

Cutting List				
Key	**Part**	**Dimension**	**Pcs.**	**Material**
A	Side panel	¾ × 17¼ × 30"	2	Plywood
B	End panel	¾ × 17¼ × 16½"	2	Plywood
C	Bottom panel	¾ × 16½ × 28½"	1	Plywood
D	Side cleat	¾ × 1½ × 28½"	2	Plywood
E	End cleat	¾ × 1½ × 15"	2	Plywood

Cutting List				
Key	**Part**	**Dimension**	**Pcs.**	**Material**
F	Bottom molding	½ × 1⅜ × *"	4	Stop molding
G	Corner molding	¼ × 1⁵⁄₁₆ × 12"	4	Corner molding
H	Lid	¾ × 18⅛ × 30⅛"	1	Plywood
I	Top cap	¾ × 1⅜ × *"	4	Shelf cap

Materials: Wood screws (#6 × 1¼", #6 × 2"), finish nails (4d), brads (¾", 1¼"), wood glue, finishing materials.

Note: Measurements reflect the actual thickness of dimensional lumber.

*Cut to fit.

Use a jig saw and straightedge guide to make the scooped "kick space" cuts in the end and side panels.

Directions: Blanket Chest

MAKE THE SIDES & ENDS. The side and end panels feature cutouts made on the bottom edges to create feet. Begin by cutting the side panels (A) and end panels (B) to size. To make the cutouts, or "kick spaces," on the bottom edges of the sides, first draw cutting lines on the sides, 2" in from one long edge. Use a compass to draw the curved cutting lines at the ends of each kick space; set the compass to draw a 2"-radius semicircle, and position the point of the compass as close to the bottom edge as possible, 5" in from the ends of the side panels. Draw the semicircles. Clamp the sides to your worksurface, and make the cutouts with a jig saw **(photo A)**, using a straightedge to guide the long straight portion of the cut. To draw the cutting lines for the kick spaces on the end panels, first draw cutting lines 2" up from one short edge. Use a compass to draw the curved cutting lines at the ends of each kick space; set the compass to draw a 2"-radius semicircle, and position the point of the compass as close to the bottom edge as possible, 4¼" in from the ends of the end panels. Draw the curved semi-circles, and make the cutouts with a jig saw. Sand the edges to smooth out any rough spots.

ASSEMBLE THE CHEST. Cleats are attached to the inside faces of the side and end panels, which are fastened together to form a basic chest. The cleats support the bottom panel of the chest, so it is important to attach them to the sides and ends with their top edges

Center the end cleats over the kick spaces, leaving ¾" at each end where the side cleats will fit.

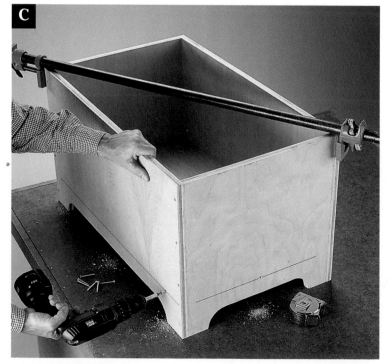

Draw opposite chest corners together with a bar or pipe clamp to keep the chest square.

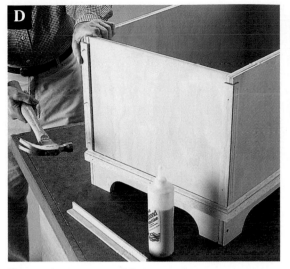

Fasten the corner molding over the corners to conceal the joints and screw heads.

Attach the top cap around the perimeter of the lid. Drive nails in partially before positioning the strips.

aligned. Cut the side cleats (D) and end cleats (E) to size. To help you position the cleats, draw reference lines on the side and end panels, 3½" up from the bottom edges and ¾" in from the side edges. Position the cleats so their top edges are flush with the reference lines, and fasten them with glue and #6 × 1¼" wood screws **(photo B),** driven through the cleats and into the panels. Countersink pilot holes in the cleats. With the cleats facing in, fasten the end panels between the side panels with glue and evenly spaced, countersunk #6 × 2" wood screws, forming a rectangular carcase. Make sure the top and bottom edges are flush, and the outside faces of the ends are flush with the side edges. Cut the bottom panel (C) to shape, and sand it smooth. Position the bottom onto the side cleats and end cleats, and clamp the panels together with a bar or pipe clamp. Check to make sure the corners of the chest are square. Unclamp the panels, apply glue to the joints and clamp them back together.

Drive countersunk #6 × 2" wood screws through the sides and ends and into the bottom edges **(photo C).** To make sure you drive the screws directly into the bottom, mark the screw centerpoints 3⅞" up from the bottoms of the sides and ends before driving the screws.

ATTACH THE MOLDING. In order to cover the screws in the sides, ends and bottom, two different types of molding pieces are attached to the chest on the corners and along the bottoms of the side and end panels. Start by cutting the bottom molding (F) from ½ × 1⅜" stop molding. Cut the strips to fit around the sides and ends, 4⅜" up from their bottom edges, miter-cutting the ends of the pieces at 45° angles so they will fit together at the corners. Position the bottom molding on the sides and ends, and use glue and 4d finish nails to fasten it. Be sure you apply glue and drive nails through the joints where the molding pieces meet to "lock-nail" the pieces. Cut the corner molding (G) into ¼ × 1⁵⁄₁₆ × 12" pieces. Use glue and ¾" brads to fasten

the corner molding over the joints between the end and side panels **(photo D).** Make sure the bottom edges of the corner molding butt against the top edges of the bottom molding. Use a nail set to recess all the nails used to fasten the molding to the chest. We sanded the bottom edges of the corner molding to meet the bottom molding. Sand the top edges of the ends and sides to smooth the edges and corners.

MAKE THE LID. Cut the lid (H) to size, and sand it smooth. Cut four pieces of top cap (I) from ¾ × 1⅜" shelf cap molding to fit around the perimeter of the lid. Use glue and 4d finish nails to attach the top cap pieces, keeping the top edges flush **(photo E).** Glue and lock-nail the mitered corner joints. Set the lid into the top opening—no hinges are used.

APPLY FINISHING TOUCHES. Use a nail set to set all the nails and brads on the chest. Fill all visible nail holes with wood putty. Finish-sand the project to smooth out any rough spots. Finish as desired. We used a gloss enamel paint.

Waste-basket

A unique decorative accent that won't go to waste.

Sure, you probably don't give wastebaskets a second thought, but they do play an important, if often overlooked, role in every home. When a small trash bin is needed for occasional paper

items, you don't want or need a giant, heavy-duty receptacle in the middle of your den. But if you go to the store to buy a wastebasket, often your only options are molded, plastic containers. This project is simple, fun to make and guaranteed to be useful.

The feature that stands out the most on the wastebasket is the use of decorative diagonal kerfs, or slots, cut into the oak plywood sides. It's an easy technique to use, and it gives the wastebasket a customized look. We also planed the legs

on the edges to soften the overall appearance and eliminate any sharp edges. A plywood bottom is fit into the project, which is designed to hold a 9"-dia. paint can or a plastic trash bag as a liner.

This is a great little project that adds character to any den or family room setting. Compact, friendly looking and unobtrusive, this wastebasket will keep paper mess in one spot and reduce clutter, while brightening an otherwise forgotten corner of the home.

CONSTRUCTION MATERIALS

Quantity	Lumber
1	¾" × 4 × 4' red oak plywood
1	1½ × 1½" × 6' red oak
1	¾ × ¾" × 3' pine stop molding

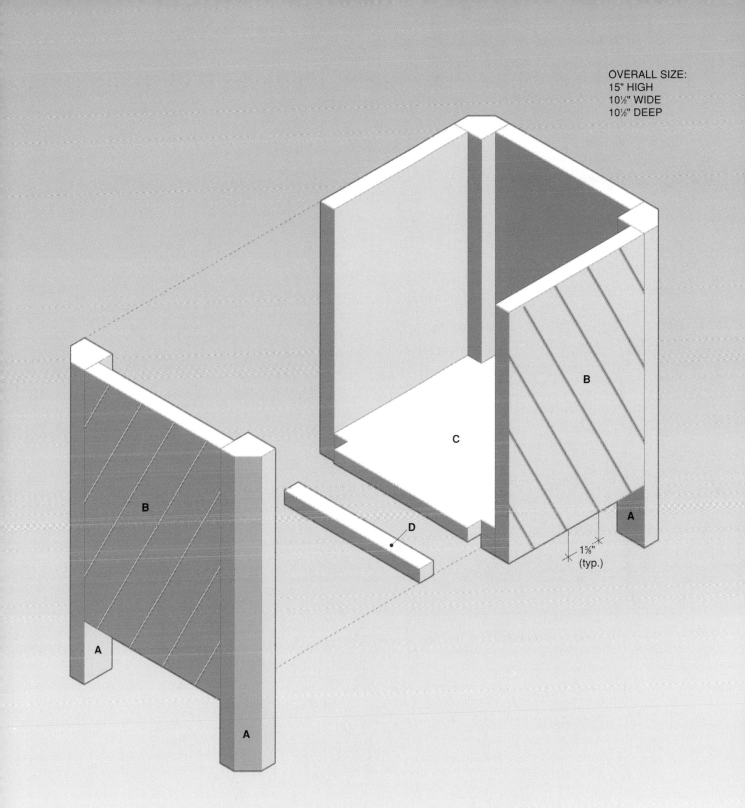

OVERALL SIZE:
15" HIGH
10½" WIDE
10½" DEEP

B

B

C

A

A

D

A

A

1⅝"
(typ.)

Key	Part	Dimension	Pcs.	Material
A	Leg	1½ × 1½ × 15"	4	Oak
B	Side panel	¾ × 7½ × 12"	4	Oak plywood

Cutting List

Key	Part	Dimension	Pcs.	Material
C	Bottom	¾ × 9 × 9"	1	Oak plywood
D	Cleat	¾ × ¾ × 7½"	4	Stop molding

Cutting List

Materials: wood glue, 4d finish nails, ¾" oak edge tape (6'), finishing materials.

Note: Measurements reflect the actual thickness of dimensional lumber.

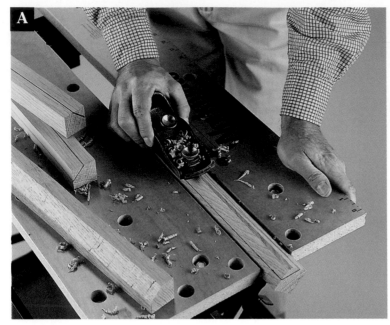

A

Use a plane to trim away one edge of each leg.

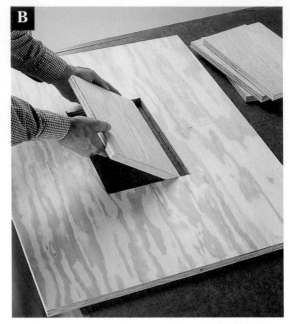

B

Use a piece of ¾" plywood with an opening the same size as a side panel as a jig for cutting kerfs.

Directions: Wastebasket

MAKE THE LEGS. Each wastebasket leg is trimmed on one edge for a decorative look. Cut the legs (A) to size from red oak 2 × 2, and sand smooth. To angle the trim cuts on the legs, use a combination square to mark lines ¾" down from one corner along two adjacent sides of each leg. Clamp a leg to your worksurface, and then use a sharp plane to remove wood evenly from the edges **(photo A).** Use a belt sander with a medium-grit sanding belt to remove the wood up to the lines and to smooth out the plane marks.

MAKE THE SIDE PANELS. Cut the side panels (B) to size from ¾"-thick oak plywood. Be careful to make sure the panels all are square and uniform in size.

MAKE THE KERF JIG. The decorative kerf cuts on the side panels are made with a circular saw and a simple jig that holds each panel for accurate cutting. The jig is made from a piece of scrap plywood approximately 24 × 32" with a cutout the size of a side panel in the center. To make the jig, center a side panel on the scrap plywood, trace around it and make the cutout with a jig saw **(photo B).**

LAY OUT THE KERF LINES. Draw cutting lines for the decorative kerfs across both the panel and the jig. To give the side panels a more interesting appearance, we cut two panels with parallel kerfs that run upward from left to right, and two

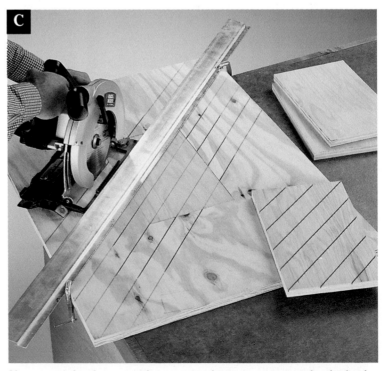

C

Use a straightedge to guide your circular saw as you make the kerf cuts in the jig and side panels.

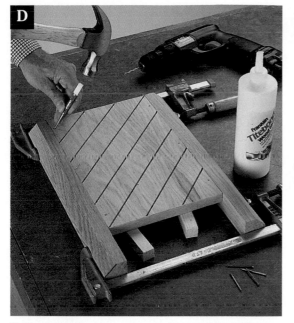

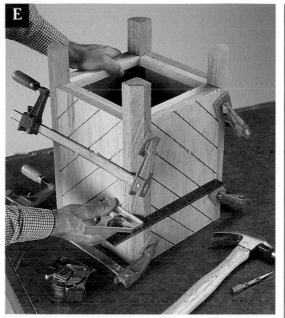

Drill pilot holes, then glue and toenail the side panels to the legs.

As you assemble the wastebasket, check frequently to make sure it's square.

with kerfs that run upward from right to left. This causes the kerfs to form peaks where the adjacent sides meet. To draw the cutting lines, set a side panel into the jig and mark points at 1⅝" intervals along the bottom edge of the panel. Draw cutting lines at a 45° angle to the bottom edge, extending the lines all the way across the panel and the jig (measure at several places to make sure all the lines are parallel). Mark each panel individually, remembering to change the direction of the lines for two of the panels.

CUT THE KERFS. Place a side panel into the jig. Clamp a long straightedge to the jig so the saw blade lines up with one cutting line. Set the blade depth at ¼", then cut along the cutting line, making sure to start and finish the cut well past the edges of the side panel. Moving the straightedge to follow the cutting lines, cut kerfs in all four side panels **(photo C).** After all side panels have been cut, use a household iron

to apply strips of self-adhesive oak veneer edge tape to the top and bottom edges of each side. Trim the edges of the tape with a utility knife when cool. Practice assembling the side panels into a box until you've figured out the pattern of the alternating panels (see *Diagram,* page 145).

ATTACH THE LEGS & SIDES. Cut the cleats (D) to size. Lay one of the side panels on top of two ¾" spacers (the cleats will work), and butt a leg against each edge. Glue and clamp the pieces together. Drill pilot holes, and toenail 4d finish nails through the side and into the legs **(photo D).** Repeat this procedure with the matching side, making sure that the pattern of the kerf cuts runs the same way. Attach the cleats to the side panels, flush with the bottom of each side panel (where the legs overhang), using glue and 4d finish nails.

ASSEMBLE THE WASTEBASKET. Assemble the basket by joining the side panels to the legs and

toenailing all the unfastened joints. Make sure the project is square **(photo E),** and that the faces of the side panels are flush with the outside of the legs. Glue and toenail the joints together with finish nails. Cut the bottom (C) to size, and cut ¾ × ¾" notches into each corner, so it will fit into the opening formed by the sides and legs. Apply glue to the tops of the cleats, and insert the bottom panel.

APPLY FINISHING TOUCHES. Sand any remaining rough edges smooth with fine-grit sandpaper. Be careful not to sand through any veneer on the side edges. Finish as desired. We left the wood unstained and applied two coats of satin-gloss polyurethane.

TIP

When planing wood, you may find that the wood can be worked more easily when planing with the grain. Don't try to remove too much wood at one time; smooth, easy strokes will achieve the best results.

Trash Can Protector

*Store that unsightly garbage can in this little structure to keep it
hidden and safe from pests.*

CONSTRUCTION MATERIALS

Quantity	Lumber
4	2" × 4 × 8' pine
1	¾" × 2 × 4' plywood
3	⅝" × 4 × 8' grooved siding
11	1 × 2" × 8' cedar

Anyone who has spent time at a cabin or a vacation home knows that garbage can storage can be a problem. Trash cans are not only ugly, they attract raccoons and other troublesome pests. Keep the trash out of sight and away from nighttime visitors with this simple trash can protector. It accommodates a 44-gallon can and features a front and top that swing open for easy access. The 2 × 4 frame is paneled with grooved plywood siding. A cedar frame and cross rail stiffens each side panel and adds a decorative touch to the project. We used construction adhesive on this project because it adapts well to varying rates of expansion.

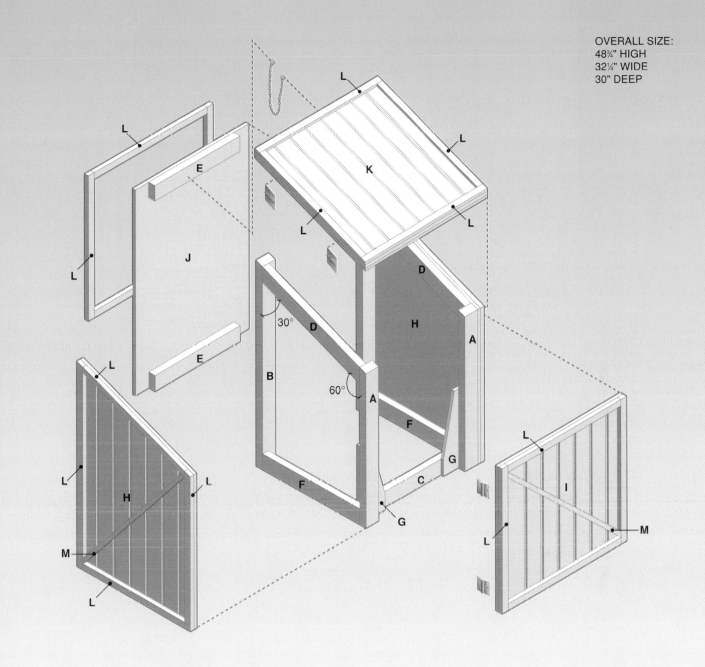

OVERALL SIZE:
48¾" HIGH
32¼" WIDE
30" DEEP

30°

60°

Cutting List

Key	Part	Dimension	Pcs.	Material
A	Front strut	1½ × 3½ × 36"	2	Pine
B	Back strut	1½ × 3½ × 46"	2	Pine
C	Front stringer	1½ × 3½ × 26¼"	1	Pine
D	Top rail	1½ × 3½ × 29¼"	2	Pine
E	Back stringer	1½ × 3½ × 22¼"	2	Pine
F	Bottom stringer	1½ × 3½ × 25½"	2	Pine
G	Brace	¾ × 6 × 16"	2	Plywood

Cutting List

Key	Part	Dimension	Pcs.	Material
H	Side panel	⅝ × 29⅛ × 45¾"	2	Plywood siding
I	Front panel	⅝ × 32¼ × 34"	1	Plywood siding
J	Back panel	⅝ × 29¼ × 45¾"	1	Plywood siding
K	Top panel	⅝ × 33¾ × 32¼"	1	Plywood siding
L	Side batten	⅞ × 1½ × *	20	Cedar
M	Cross rail	⅞ × 1½ × *	4	Cedar

Materials: Construction adhesive, deck screws (1¼", 2", 3"), 1" panhead screws (2), galvanized finish nails (6d), 3 × 3" utility hinges (2), 3 × 3" spring-loaded hinges (2), galvanized steel or plastic door pulls (2), steel chain (28"), finishing materials.

Note: Measurements reflect the actual thickness of dimensional lumber.
*Cut to fit.

Make sure the back stringer is centered and flush with the bottom edge of the back before attaching it with screws and panel adhesive.

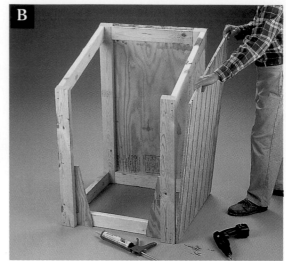

Attach side panels to the frame, making sure the front and top edges are flush with the frame.

Directions:
Trash Can Protector

MAKE THE BACK PANEL. Start by cutting the back panel (J) to size from grooved plywood siding. Then cut the back stringers (E) to size. Position one back stringer on the ungrooved face of the back panel, flush with the bottom edge. Center the back stringer on the back panel: each end of the back stringer should be 3½" in from the back panel sides. Attach the stringer with construction adhesive and 1¼" deck screws **(photo A).** Center the remaining back stringer on the back panel, ¾" down from the top edge, and attach it.

MAKE THE SIDE FRAMES. The sides are simple 2 × 4 frames attached to plywood panels. The frames slant downward from back to front at a 30° angle. Begin by setting a circular saw or a power miter box to cut at a 30° angle. Cut the front strut (A) and back strut (B) to length, making sure one end of each front and back strut is cut at a 30° angle. This slanted end cut should not affect the over-

all length of the struts (see *Diagram*, page 149). Cut the bottom stringers (F) to length. Position the front struts on edge on your worksurface. Butt the end of a bottom stringer against each front strut. The outside faces of the bottom stringers should be flush with the outside edges of the front struts, and flush with the square ends of the front struts. Apply construction adhesive, and drive 3" deck screws through the front struts and into the ends of the bottom stringers. Make sure the tops of the front struts slant in the same direction. Position a back strut against the unattached end of each bottom stringer, and attach them, making sure the slanted top ends of the back struts are facing the front struts. Next, cut the top rails (D) to length. In order for the top rails to fit between the front struts and back struts, their ends must be cut at a 60° angle. When you cut the ends, make sure they are slanted in the correct directions. (You may find it easiest to hold the top rails in place against the front and back struts, and trace

the angle directly onto the top rails.) Position the top rails between the front struts and back struts, making sure the outside faces are flush with the outside edges of the front struts and back struts. Attach the top rails with construction adhesive and 3" deck screws.

MAKE & ATTACH THE SIDE BRACES. The braces strengthen the frame and fit just behind the front struts, flush with the bottom stringers. Cut the braces (G) to size. Cut a slanted profile on the braces, so the top edge is 3" long and the bottom edge is 6" long. This slanted profile leaves room to move a garbage can in and out of the unit. Position the braces against the inside faces of the front struts, making sure the braces butt against the bottom stringers. Fasten the braces with construction adhesive and 2" deck screws.

JOIN THE SIDES. The two side frames are now joined to create a rough box frame. Start by cutting the front stringer (C) to length. Stand the side frames up on your worksurface so the front struts face the same direc-

Mark the ends of the cross rails before cutting them to fit between the frame corners.

tion. Position the front stringer between the side frames with one face butting against each brace. Make sure the ends of the front stringer are in contact with the bottom stringers, and attach the front stringer with construction adhesive and 3" deck screws.

COMPLETE THE FRAME. Position the back panel against the frame sides. Make sure the back stringers are flush against the back struts, and attach the back panel to the frame with construction adhesive and 1¼" deck screws. The side edges of the back should be flush with the frame sides. Cut the side panels (H) to the size shown in the *Cutting List*. Set the side panels against the frame sides, making sure the front and rear edges align and the panel is resting squarely on the ground. Trace the top edge of the frame onto the back (ungrooved) face of the side panels. Cut along the line with a circular saw. Attach the side panels with construction adhesive and screws **(photo B).**

ATTACH THE BATTENS & CROSS RAILS. The battens are pieces of trim that frame the panels along their edges. The cross rails fit diagonally from corner to corner on the side panels. Measure the sides carefully before cutting the battens to length. Cut the battens (L) to fit along the side and back panel edges. Once the battens have been cut to length, fasten them to the side panels with construction adhesive and 6d finish nails. Position the diagonal side battens on the sides so they span from corner to corner. Mark the angle required for the ends to fit snugly into the corners **(photo C).** Cut the cross rails to size and attach them. The back battens form a simple frame around the back. Attach the back battens, making sure their outside and top edges are flush with the side faces and top edges of the rear side battens.

MAKE THE TOP & FRONT PANELS. The top and front panels are framed in the same way as the side panels and back panels. Start by cutting the top panel (K) and front panel (I) to size from grooved plywood siding. Cut these parts from the same sheet of siding to make sure the grooves align on the finished project. Cut battens to frame the edges of the top panel on both faces, then at-

tach battens on the front panel. Like the side panels, the front panel is framed on one face only, and has a cross rail stretching from corner to corner. Attach two spring-loaded, self-closing hinges to the front panel, and mount it on the front of the project. The bottom edge of the front panel should be 1" up from the bottoms of the stringers. Mount the top panel with two 3 × 3" utility hinges **(photo D).** Attach handles or pulls on the front and top of the garbage can holder. Use two panhead screws to attach a 28"-long safety chain to the back edge of the back stringer and top panel to keep the top panel from swinging open too far. Fasten the ends of the chain 10" in from the hinged edge of the top panel. Finish the trash can protector with an exterior-rated stain. If pests are a serious problem, attach latches to the front and top to hold them in place.

Mount the top to the top of a side panel with 3 × 3" utility hinges.

151

Sports Locker

Whether your game is basketball, skiing, golf, hockey, baseball or cricket, this roomy sports locker will become a most valuable project.

PROJECT
POWER TOOLS

I f you or your children are active in sports like golf, baseball, hockey or basketball, then you can imagine how valuable a good sports locker can be. Six feet tall and broad in the shoulders, this

locker can handle just about anything you throw at it. But don't be afraid that this storage project will make your house smell like a locker room—the pegboard doors provide plenty of ventilation inside the locker.

If, like most people, your interest in sports is confined to a few activities, you can easily customize this sports locker to meet your needs. Add extra shelves to store more smaller-scale equipment or outdoor clothing; if you play a lot of softball, put an extra row of bat

hangers in the open side; if you are an outdoorsman, replace the bat hangers with a piece of closet rod so you can store your hunting or fishing apparel in one location (where it won't pass its outdoorsy fragrance along to your other outerwear); if your family enjoys golf, eliminate the bottom two shelves to create space for two more sets of clubs. By using a little imagination, you can turn this versatile project into a real team player.

CONSTRUCTION MATERIALS

Quantity	Lumber
2	¾" × 4 × 8' plywood
1	¼" × 4 × 8' plywood
1	2 × 4" × 6' pine
6	1 × 2" × 6' pine
1	⅛" × 4 × 8' pegboard
4	½ × 1⅛" × 8' wainscot cap

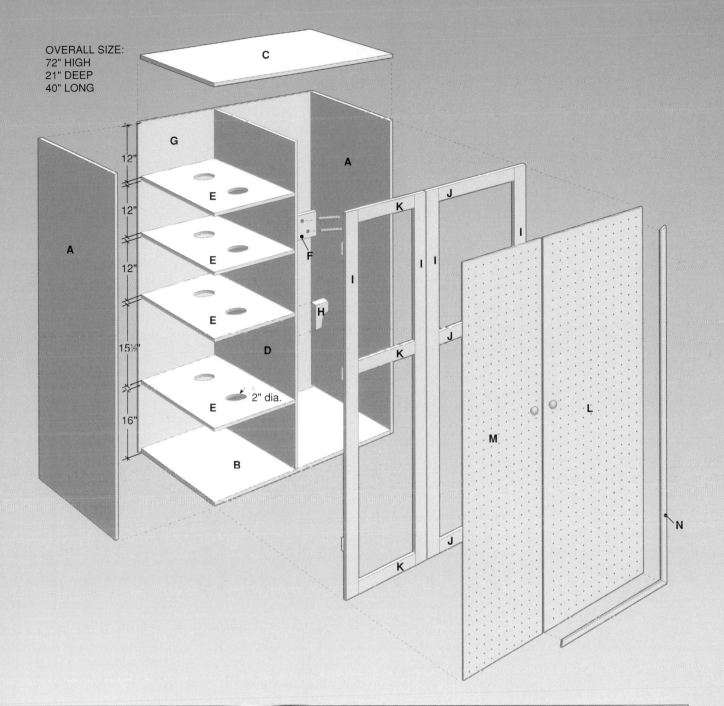

OVERALL SIZE:
72" HIGH
21" DEEP
40" LONG

2" dia.

Cutting List				
Key	**Part**	**Dimension**	**Pcs.**	**Material**
A	Side	¾ × 20 × 71¼"	2	Plywood
B	Bottom	¾ × 20 × 38½"	1	Plywood
C	Top	¾ × 20 × 40"	1	Plywood
D	Divider	¾ × 20 × 70½"	1	Plywood
E	Shelf	¾ × 16 × 20"	4	Plywood
F	Stretcher	¾ × 6 × 21¾"	1	Plywood
G	Back	¼ × 40 × 72"	1	Plywood

Cutting List				
Key	**Part**	**Dimension**	**Pcs.**	**Material**
H	Hanger	1½ × 3½ × 4"	8	Pine
I	Door stile	¾ × 1½ × 71¼"	4	Pine
J	Long rail	¾ × 1½ × 19¹³⁄₁₆"	3	Pine
K	Short rail	¾ × 1½ × 14¹⁄₁₆"	3	Pine
L	Wide door	⅛ × 22¾ × 71¼"	1	Pegboard
M	Narrow door	⅛ × 17 × 71¼"	1	Pegboard
N	Door trim	½ × 1⅛ × *	8	Molding

Materials: Glue, 2" wainscot cap molding (32'), wood screws (#6 × 2", #8 × ¾"), 1" wire nails, 1½ × 2" butt hinges (4), door pulls or handles (2), magnetic door catches (4), Shaker-style pegs (8), finishing materials.

Note: Measurements reflect the actual size of dimensional lumber.

*Cut to fit

Install the divider panel between the top and bottom panels, separating the locker into an open area and a shelf area.

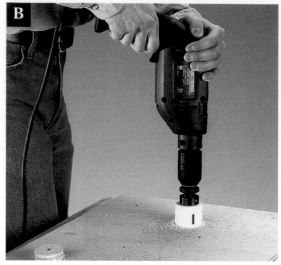

Using a hole saw, cut 2"-dia. holes in the shelves to keep balls from rolling inside the locker.

Use wood spacers to support each shelf while you fasten it with screws.

Directions:
Sports Locker

BUILD THE FRAME. The sports locker is basically a plywood box with a divider panel and shelves. Start by cutting the components of the box: the sides (A), bottom (B) and top (C) from ¾"-thick plywood.

Sand the surfaces with medium (100- or 120-grit) sandpaper to smooth out the rough spots, then fasten the bottom between the sides with glue and #6 × 2" wood screws. Counterbore the pilot holes for the screws deep enough to fill with wood putty to cover the screw heads. Attach the top to the sides with glue and screws driven down through the top and into the top edges of the side panels. Cut the divider (D) to size. Lay the box you've assembled on its back edge, and fasten the divider between the top and bottom panels of the box, 16" from the inside of the left side panel **(photo A).** Make sure the back and front edges of the divider are flush with the edges of the top and bottom panels.

BUILD THE SHELVES. Our project has four shelves, but if you prefer you may customize your sports locker to match your storage needs by adding shelves or rearranging their positions. Cut the shelves (E) to size. Because we wanted this sports locker to be able to store balls without having them roll all over the locker, we used a

2"-dia. hole saw mounted on an electric drill to drill holes in the shelves. When set in the holes, round objects remain stationary. Cut two holes in each shelf, centered from side to side, with centerpoints 5" from the front and back shelf edges **(photo B).** When using a hole saw, place a piece of scrap wood under the project to prevent damage to your worksurface. Smooth out the edges on the shelves, and sand any rough surfaces.

ATTACH THE SHELVES AND BACK. Mark the shelf locations on the side and divider (see *Diagram*, page 153). Cut four scraps of wood the same length as the shelf height to use as spacers to support each shelf while you install it. Install the shelves by driving #6 × 2" screws through the left side and the divider, and into the edges of the shelves **(photo C).** Cut the back (G) to size. Fasten it to the sides, top and bottom with evenly spaced 1" wire nails. Nail along one side first, then square the frame before nailing the remaining edges.

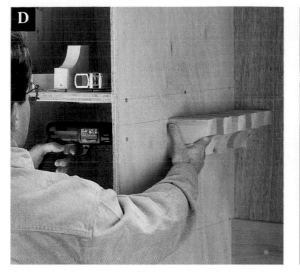

Attach the hangers by driving screws through the divider and into the ends of the hangers.

Assemble the rails and stiles to make the two different-size door frames.

ATTACH THE STRETCHER. The stretcher fits at the back of the open section of the sports locker to fortify the side-to-side strength and provide a mounting surface for pegs. Cut the stretcher (F) to size from ¾" plywood. Drill holes for Shaker-style pegs in the stretcher, making sure the holes match the diameter of the pegs. We installed two staggered rows of pegs at 8" intervals. Mark a horizontal reference line for positioning the top of the stretcher, 39" up from the bottom panel. Attach the stretcher with wood screws driven through the side and divider panels, and into the ends of the stretcher.

ATTACH THE HANGERS. We installed two rows of 2 × 4 hangers that are designed to store everything from baseball bats to canoe paddles. Cut 8 hangers (H) to size from 2 × 4 pine. Set the legs of a compass to a 2" radius, and position the point of the compass at one corner of each hanger. Draw a ¼-round cutting line at the corner, then cut along the line with a jig saw. Sand the cut

smooth. Draw reference lines for two rows of hangers 30" and 52" up from the bottom panel. Space the hangers so they are 1¼" apart—a good distance for hanging bats or paddles between the hangers. Fasten the pieces by driving two screws through the divider and into each hanger **(photo D).**

BUILD THE DOORS. The two locker doors are sized so the gap where they meet falls over the divider panel. Cut the door stiles (I), long rails (J) and short rails (K) from 1 × 2 pine. Cut the wide door (L) and narrow door (M) to size from ⅛"-thick pegboard. Apply glue to the ends of the rails, and fasten the rails between the stiles by driving wood screws through the stiles and into the rails **(photo E),** completing the door frames. Position the pegboard panels over the door frames, making sure they don't overhang. Screw the panels to the frames with ¾"-long wood screws, keeping the frames square with the panels as you go. Finally, miter-cut 2" wainscot cap molding (N) to fit around the edges of each door.

Tape the cap pieces to the door so they hold their position, then drill pilot holes through the pieces and the pegboard. Attach the cap frame to the doors with glue and 1" wire nails.

APPLY THE FINISHING TOUCHES. Fill all screw holes and exposed plywood edges with wood putty, and sand all rough edges and surfaces smooth. Apply glue to the tips of the pegs and insert them into the stretcher. Prime and paint the locker—we used enamel paint for a hard finish. Hang the doors with two 1½ × 2" butt hinges per door, then attach a pull or handle to each door. Install magnetic door catches for each door at the top and bottom of the divider.

TIP

Pegboard can be tricky to paint with a brush or roller—no matter how hard you try, the peg holes always seem to clog with paint, creating a ragged appearance. For best results, paint pegboard with spray paint or a paint sprayer.

Rod & Tackle Center

*This two-sided equip-
ment storage center
can hold up to eight
fishing rods, plus
spare tackle and a
pair of tackle boxes.*

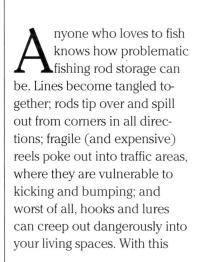

Anyone who loves to fish knows how problematic fishing rod storage can be. Lines become tangled together; rods tip over and spill out from corners in all directions; fragile (and expensive) reels poke out into traffic areas, where they are vulnerable to kicking and bumping; and worst of all, hooks and lures can creep out dangerously into your living spaces. With this simple storage center, you can keep your fishing rods and tackle well organized, tangle-free and out of harm's way.

Designed with a sleek profile so it fits against a wall, this rod & tackle center makes efficient use of your space. The slide-out tackle tray and the open tackle box storage area can be accessed from either side. The rod racks feature cutouts in both the upper and lower racks so rods will not slip out or rub together.

The rod & tackle center can be positioned flat against the wall to consume the minimum amount of floor space, or you can set it with a side panel against the wall for maximum accessibility. Either way, at least one side panel will be exposed so you can attach hooks for hanging landing nets or even your favorite fishing hat.

CONSTRUCTION MATERIALS

Quantity	Lumber
1	¾" × 4 × 8' plywood
1	¼" × 2 × 2' lauan plywood

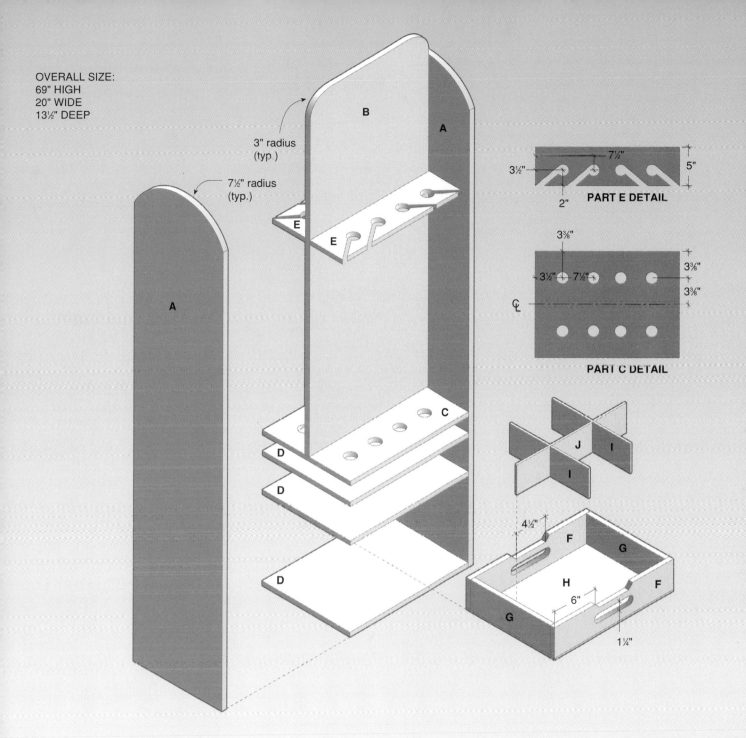

OVERALL SIZE:
69" HIGH
20" WIDE
13½" DEEP

3" radius (typ.)

7½" radius (typ.)

B

A

A

E

E

C

D

D

D

J

I

I

F

G

H

F

G

4½"

6"

1¼"

PART E DETAIL

7½"

3½"

2"

5"

PART C DETAIL

3⅜"

3½"

7½"

3⅜"

3⅜"

C̸L

Key	Part	Dimension	Pcs.	Material
A	Side	¾ × 13½ × 65¼"	2	Plywood
B	Divider	¾ × 18½ × 48"	1	Plywood
C	Lower rack	¾ × 13½ × 18½"	1	Plywood
D	Shelf	¾ × 13½ × 18½"	3	Plywood
E	Upper rack	¾ × 5 × 18½"	2	Plywood

Cutting List

Key	Part	Dimension	Pcs.	Material
F	Tray front/back	¾ × 4⅛ × 18¼"	2	Plywood
G	Tray side	¾ × 4⅛ × 11½"	2	Plywood
H	Tray bottom	¼ × 13 × 18¼"	1	Lauan plywood
I	Short tray divider	¼ × 4 × 11½"	2	Lauan plywood
J	Long tray divider	¼ × 4 × 16¾"	1	Lauan plywood

Cutting List

Materials: Glue, #6 × 1⅝" deck screws, ¾" wire brads, finishing materials.

Note: Measurements reflect the actual thickness of dimensional lumber.

Use a jig saw to cut the 7½"-radius curves on the tops of the side panels.

centerpoint, and drill a small pilot hole at the second point. Next, mark a centerpoint on each side panel, 7½" down from the top and centered side to side. Drive a finish nail through the small pilot hole in the compass and into one of the side panels at the center-point. Insert a pencil into the ¼"-dia. hole, and draw the roundover using the finish nail as a pivot point. Draw roundovers on both side panels. Cut along the roundover lines on both panels with a jig saw **(photo A).** Sand out any rough spots on the side panels.

ATTACH THE SHELVES. The rod & tackle center has four shelves installed near the bottom. The bottom shelf is flush with the bottoms of the side panels; the second shelf supports the slid-ing tray; the third shelf supports the ends of the fishing rod handles; and the fourth shelf features round cutouts to hold the handles in place. Start by cutting the lower rack (C) and shelves (D) to size. Mark cen-terpoints for two rows of four

Directions:
Rod & Tackle Center

MAKE THE SIDES. The sides are the standards that support the shelves and racks in the rod & tackle center. They feature decorative roundovers on top to make the appearance less bulky. Start by cutting the sides (A) to size from ¾"-thick ply-wood (we used birch plywood because it's easier to work with

and finish than most grades of pine plywood). Draw a 7½"-radius roundover at the top of each side panel. If you don't have a compass that is large enough to draw a curve that big, make one yourself: first, cut a narrow strip of scrap wood about 10" long. Then, mark a centerpoint on the scrap near one end, and an-other 7½" in from the first point. Drill a ¼"-dia. hole at the first

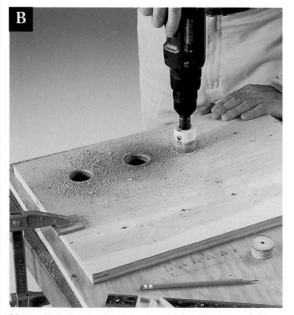

Use a 1½"-dia. hole saw attachment in your drill to cut evenly spaced holes in the lower rack.

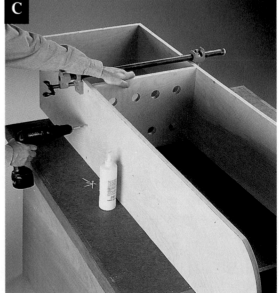

Glue and clamp the lower rack between the sides, then reinforce the joint with wood screws.

158

1½"-dia. holes on the lower shelf, according to the positioning shown on the *Part C Detail* on page 157. Cut the holes with a 1½"-dia. hole saw attachment and drill **(photo B).** Set the sides on edge, about 20" apart. Apply glue to the edges of one shelf, and position it between the sides so the bottom face is flush with the bottom edges of the sides. Drill countersunk pilot holes, and drive #6 × 1⅝" wood screws through the sides and into the shelf. Next, glue and clamp the lower rack between the sides, 20" up from the bottoms. Drive #6 × 1⅝" wood screws to reinforce the joint **(photo C).** Install the remaining two crosspieces with glue and countersunk deck screws. The bottoms should be 12" and 17½" up from the bottoms of the side panels.

INSTALL THE DIVIDER. The divider fits between the side panels, resting on top of the lower rack. Cut the divider (B) to size. Use a compass to draw 3" radius roundovers on both corners at one end (the top) of the divider. Cut the roundovers with a jig saw. Apply beads of glue to the bottom (square) edge of the divider and the outer edges, then position it so it is centered between the side panels, front to back, and resting squarely on the top of the lower rack. Clamp the divider between the sides with pipe clamps or bar clamps **(photo D),** then drive wood screws through countersunk pilot holes in the side panels and into the edges of the divider— space the screws at 8" intervals.

INSTALL THE UPPER RACKS. The upper racks are installed on each side of the divider to create slip-in supports for the

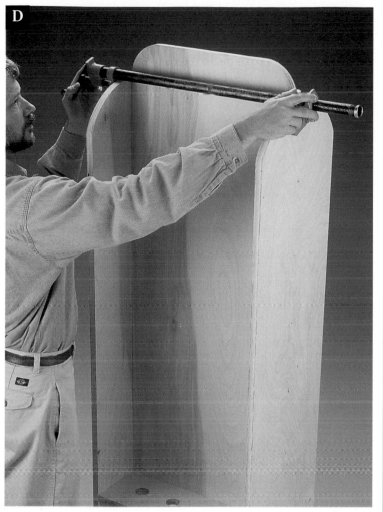

Clamp the side panels around the divider after you install the shelves and lower rack.

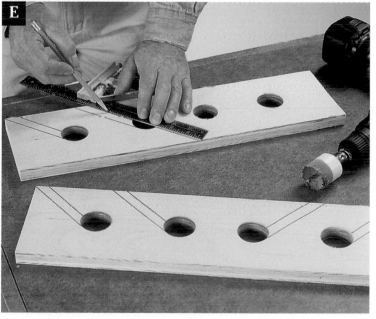

Lay out the angled slots that connect the holes to the front edges of the upper racks, where the tips of your fishing rods will fit.

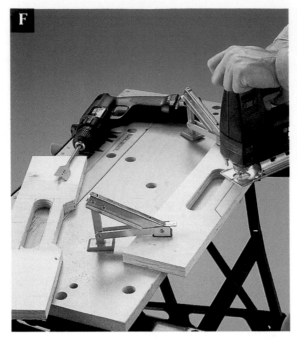

Cut access notches and finger-grip cutouts into the front and back boards of the tray.

The tray dividers are notched to form half-lap joints—test to make sure they fit together before you glue them into the tray.

tips of the fishing rods. Both upper rack boards have a row of four 1½"-dia. holes, with an angled slot cut from the front edge of each board to each hole so you can slip the fishing rod into the hole. Cut the upper racks (E) to size, and mark centerpoints for four evenly spaced 1½" holes in each shelf, according to the spacing shown in *Part E Detail* on page 157. Also draw cutting lines to mark angled, ½"-wide slots from the front edge of each rack to each hole **(photo E).** Cut the slots with a jig saw. To attach the upper racks, mark straight reference lines on both faces of the divider, 28" up from the lower rack. Position the upper racks between the side panels so the tops are flush with the reference lines. Make sure the upper racks butt flush against the divider. Drill countersunk pilot holes through the sides, and attach the upper racks with glue and countersunk #6 × 1⅝" wood

screws driven through the sides and into the ends of the racks.

MAKE THE TRAY BOX. The box that serves as the tackle tray has a front and back with access notches and slots for finger-grips. Cut the tray front/back boards (F), the tray sides (G) and the tray bottom (H). Mark a centerline on the faces of the front and back boards, measuring from end to end. Draw a 1¼"-high × 6¼"-long cutout on each board. The tip of the cutout should be 2¼" down from the top of the board. Use a drill with a 1¼" spade bit to create the rounded ends of the cut, then connect the holes with a jig saw to form the slot on each board. Then, cut a ¾"-deep notch in the top edge, centered on the centerline, starting 6" in from each end of the board. The sides of the notch should angle in at about 45° **(photo F).** Drill pilot holes, and attach the tray sides between the tray front and back with glue and #6 × 1⅝"

wood screws, forming a rectangular frame. Attach the tray bottom to the frame with glue and ¾" wire brads.

INSTALL THE TRAY DIVIDER. The tray dividers are made from thin lauan plywood, cut in strips that fit together with half-lap joints. Cut the tray dividers (I, J) to size from ¼"-thick lauan plywood. Use a jig saw to cut a ¼"-wide × 2"-long notch in the center of each of the two shorter dividers (I). Cut a pair of ¼"-wide × 2"-long notches in the longer divider (J), 5¼" in from each end. Fit a short divider notch over each long divider notch to make sure the parts fit together **(photo G)**, then glue them in place in the bottom of the tray.

APPLY FINISHING TOUCHES. Fill all screw holes with putty. Finish-sand the entire project, and apply a paint and primer finish. Paint the tray section separately, then insert it in the shelf area when the finish has completely dried.